Organizing and Editing Your Photos with Picasa

Visual QuickProject Guide

by Steve Schwartz

Peachpit Press

Visual QuickProject Guide
Organizing and Editing Your Photos with Picasa
Steve Schwartz

Peachpit Press

1249 Eighth Street
Berkeley, CA 94710
510/524-2178
800/283-9444
510/524-2221 (fax)

Find us on the World Wide Web at: www.peachpit.com
To report errors, please send a note to errata@peachpit.com
Peachpit Press is a division of Pearson Education

Editor: Suzie Nasol
Production: Lisa Brazieal
Compositor: Steve Schwartz
Cover design: The Visual Group with Aren Howell
Cover photo credit: Dynamic Graphics
Interior design: Elizabeth Castro
Indexer: FireCrystal Communications

Notice of Liability
The information in this book is distributed on an "As Is" basis, without warranty. While every precaution has been taken in the preparation of the book, neither the author nor Peachpit Press shall have any liability to any person or entity with respect to any loss or damage caused or alleged to be caused directly or indirectly by the instructions contained in this book or by the computer software and hardware products described in it.

Trademarks
Visual QuickProject Guide is a registered trademark of Peachpit Press, a division of Pearson Education.

Throughout this book, trademarks are used. Rather than put a trademark symbol with every occurrence of a trademarked name, we state that we are using the names in an editorial fashion only and to the benefit of the trademark owner with no intention of infringement of the trademark. No such use, or the use of any trade name, is intended to convey endorsement or other affiliation with this book.

ISBN 0-321-36901-7

9 8 7 6 5 4 3 2 1

Printed and bound in the United States of America

To all my wonderful friends
at Peachpit Press

Special Thanks to...

Cliff Colby and Nancy Davis of Peachpit Press for encouraging me to write this book devoted to Picasa.

Suzie Nasol and Lisa Brazieal of Peachpit Press for their dedication to making this the best book possible.

Emily Glossbrenner of FireCrystal Communications for creating another exceptional index.

The Peachpit employees and my friends who were kind enough to provide their personal photos for use in this book.

contents

contents

contents

introduction

The Visual QuickProject Guide that you hold in your hands offers a unique way to learn about new technologies. Instead of drowning you in theoretical possibilities and lengthy explanations, this Visual QuickProject Guide uses big, color illustrations coupled with clear, concise step-by-step instructions to show you how to easily complete tasks and projects.

Picasa 2, a free download from Google (www.google.com), is a multi-purpose program. First, you can use it to take control of and organize all the digital images on your hard disk, CDs, and DVDs. It doesn't matter where the images originally came from—whether they were taken with a digital camera, scanned, received in email, or downloaded from the Web. All are fair game to Picasa.

Next, you can use Picasa to edit images. By applying Picasa's tools, you can adjust contrast and color, crop and straighten photos, correct red eye, and apply filters to change an image's feel, for example.

Finally, Picasa can help you preserve and share your pictures with others. You can create backups, print on popular photo papers, email pictures to your friends, and swap images using Hello (a free chat utility from Google). And if you register and create a free blog (Web log) with Blogger, you can use the Picasa/Hello combination to upload images to your blog.

Unlike most books in this series, this one's focus isn't projects. Instead, this book is designed to give you a solid understanding of Picasa 2 and its many capabilities. This colorful, friendly guide is your first step in putting Picasa to work for you. Happy organizing, editing, and picture sharing!

what you'll learn

Chapters 1 and 2. Before you get started exploring Picasa, the first step is to install your free copy of the software. In Chapter 1, you'll be stepped through the process of downloading and installing Picasa. If you'd like to take advantage of some related software, you'll also find out how to download and install Hello (a free photo chat program), as well as register with Blogger to create a free blog. In Chapter 2, you'll learn about Picasa's capabilities, explore the program interface, set preferences for the way the program works, and use the Help system.

A folder in the Picture Library

Chapter 3. This chapter discusses viewing your photos. You'll learn about the Picture Library—working with thumbnails, sorting the Folder List and files in folders, and searching for photos. To view selected thumbnails, you can open them for editing (in Picasa or another program), display them as a slide show, or use Timeline view to view them in date order.

Chapter 4. Next, you'll learn about Picasa's image organization features. Like most computer users, your hard disk is probably filled with photos and other images. You can use Picasa to organize picture folders into collections of similar images (such as all the ones of friends), group individual photos into labels (all images of your son, regardless of the folder in which they're stored), assign keywords to images to classify and make them easier to find, and add text captions to photos. You'll also learn how to store new image files and folders in Picasa, as well as to import photos from a digital camera.

Folder List

Tuning tools

Chapter 5. In this chapter, you'll learn about Picasa's editing features. You can use the Auto tools to instantly correct contrast and color. And you can manually crop and straighten photos, as well as fix red eye in flash shots.

If you need more precise image-correction capabilities, you can use the Tuning tools to simultaneously adjust the contrast, color, and lighting.

Picasa also has batch edit controls you can use to apply an edit to multiple pictures.

Chapter 6. Here you'll learn about applying filters to your photos, sharpening pictures, and turning color shots into black-and-white or sepia-tone images, for example.

Original photo

Sepia filter applied

what you'll learn (cont.)

Chapter 7. In this chapter, you'll learn about Picasa's impressive printing and emailing capabilities. Picasa can print pictures on many common paper sizes, automatically resizing each image as needed. The Review function instantly tells you whether a given photo has sufficient resolution to print acceptably at the chosen size. The email feature helps you send photos from your Picture Library to friends and relatives.

You can even print a contact sheet for any folder to document its contents.

Chapter 8. This chapter shows some fun projects you can make with Picasa. You can use your personal photos to create a Windows Desktop or screen saver, make a slideshow-style movie, design posters and collages, and generate a Web page so you can display your favorite photos online.

Photo collage

Chapter 9. Edits made in Picasa never alter the original file. However, if you need to move pictures to another computer or open them in another program, this chapter will show you how to save and export your edited images. You'll also learn to back up your photos and compile gift CDs to share selected images with family and friends.

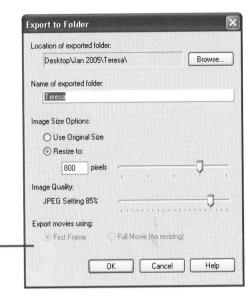

When exporting edited pictures from Picasa, you can optionally change their size and quality.

Chapter 10. In this chapter, you'll learn to use Hello to chat on the Internet with friends and exchange photos with each other.

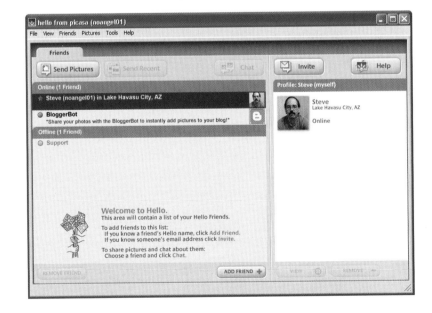

Hello chat window

how this book works

Each section begins with a descriptive title.

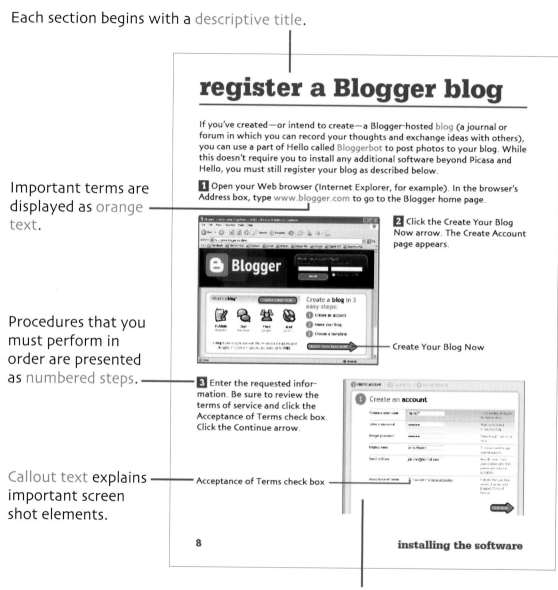

Important terms are displayed as orange text.

Procedures that you must perform in order are presented as numbered steps.

Callout text explains important screen shot elements.

Illustrative screen shots show what you'll see on your monitor or what you need to do.

An extra bits section at the end of each chapter contains tips and tricks you might like to know, but that aren't absolutely necessary for working with Picasa.

The heading for each set of tips matches the section title.

Each chapter section referred to in Extra Bits is indicated by a different colored block.

extra bits

save a copy p. 102
- The Save a Copy command has no options. No dialog box appears when saving a copy of a file in this manner. You can't specify a filename or select a destination folder, for example.
- You can also use the Save a Copy command to simultaneously make copies of multiple pictures. Before issuing the command, [Ctrl]-click each picture that you want to copy. (When selecting pictures to copy, use Hold to add pictures from multiple folders.)

export to folder p. 103
- JPEG files use lossy compression. That is, the higher the compression you select, the more image quality you'll lose. (By comparison, compression algorithms for TIFF files are lossless. That is, no image quality is lost; the files are simply made smaller.) If you're exporting digital photos that will only be viewed onscreen, you can safely apply much higher compression before its effects are evident onscreen. However, if you intend to print the exported files or edit them in another program, you'll want to keep compression to a minimum—use a JPEG setting close to 100%.

- If you've previously exported images from the current folder, you can select the previous destination folder. Doing so prevents the creation of a new subfolder.

create a gift CD p. 106
- Gift CDs reflect edits you've made in Picasa. The resulting images can be viewed in any program—not just Picasa.
- When creating a gift CD, Picasa tells you how much data will be written and the number of discs required. A blank CD holds approximately 650 MB. If you're over that amount, you can pick a smaller image size or reduce the number of images by selecting fewer folders.

archive photos p. 108
- The advantage of backing up to a hard disk is that it occurs immediately; no disc shuffling is required. The disadvantage is that if something happens to your computer—it's stolen or destroyed, for example—your backups will be lost, too.
- When performing subsequent backups to the same set, you can add more folders by clicking their check boxes.

110 saving and backing up photos

The page number on which the section begins is shown beside the heading.

introduction

go to the Web site

While there are no materials you need to download in order to perform the tasks and procedures in this book, you may want to visit my office Web site. Any errors in this book that I uncover—and their fixes—can be viewed by going to the Errata section of the site at http://www.siliconwasteland.com/errata.htm.

Click here to go to the Errata main page

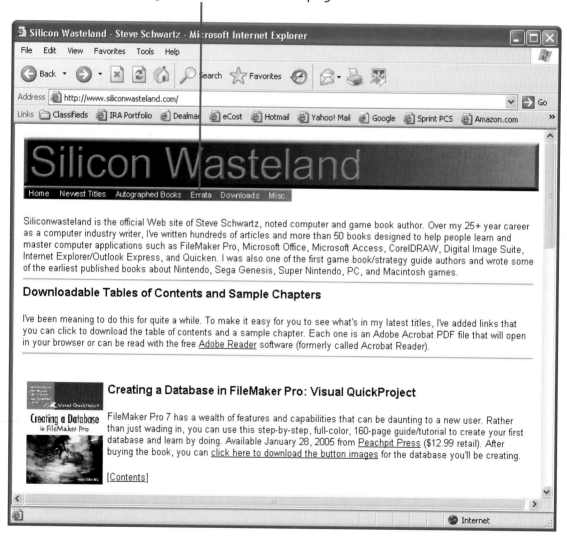

1. installing the software

This chapter explains how to download and install Picasa 2, register and download Hello, and register and create a free blog (Web log) with Blogger. Installing Hello and creating a blog are optional; neither is required in order to install or use Picasa 2.

You'll find Picasa to be a capable program for organizing all your digital images, as well as making basic edits to them.

You can use Hello (another free Picasa program) to chat, swap photos over the Internet, and post pictures to your blog.

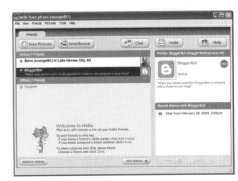

install Picasa 2

If you haven't downloaded and installed Picasa 2, follow these directions:

1 Open your Web browser (Internet Explorer, for example). In the browser's Address box, type www.picasa.com to go to the Picasa 2 home page.

You can also reach this page by visiting Google (www.google.com), clicking the More link, and then clicking the Picasa Photo Organizer icon.

2 Click the Free Download button.

Web site address

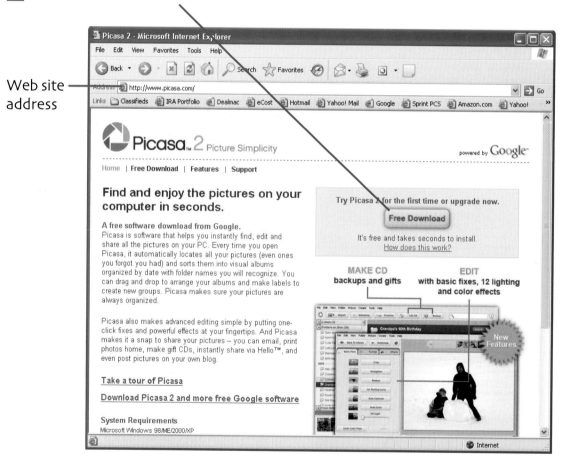

installing the software

3 In the dialog box that appears, you'll be asked whether you want to run or save the file (the Picasa installation program) you're about to download. Click the Save button.

Save the installation program. ——

4 In the Save As dialog box, select a disk location in which to save the file and then click Save. (Select an easy-to-find location, such as the Desktop.)

Save the installation program in this location/folder.

installing the software

install Picasa 2 (cont.)

5 As the file downloads to your computer, you can watch its progress in this dialog box. When the download finishes, close the dialog box (if it doesn't close by itself).

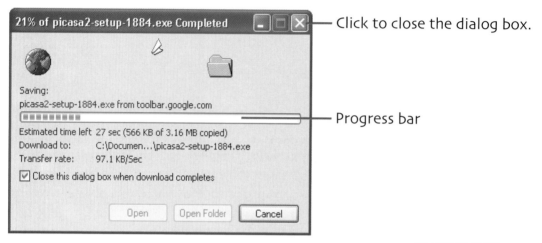 —— Click to close the dialog box.

—— Progress bar

6 To run Picasa's installation program, click (or double-click) the downloaded file's icon.

7 If you're running Windows XP, this warning dialog box will appear. Click Run to continue.

8 The Picasa 2 Setup wizard appears, open to the License Agreement screen. Click I Agree to continue.

9 On the Choose Install Location screen, specify the hard disk folder in which to install Picasa. To accept the proposed (default) folder, click Install.

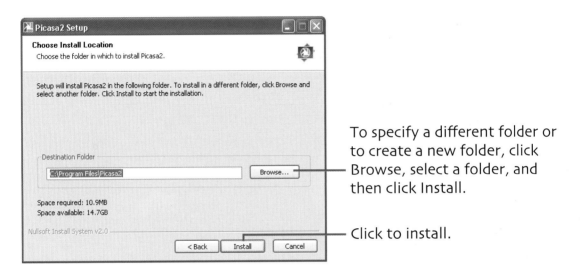

To specify a different folder or to create a new folder, click Browse, select a folder, and then click Install.

Click to install.

10 On this final screen, click check boxes to set any desired options and then click Finish.

Create Shortcut on Desktop. Add a Picasa 2 icon to the Desktop.

Add Shortcut to QuickLaunch. Add a Picasa 2 launch icon to the right of the Start button.

Show System Tray Icon at Startup. Automatically load Picasa 2 and display its icon in the System Tray (right side of the taskbar) at every startup.

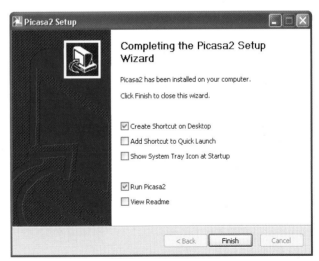

installing the software

install Hello

Hello is a dedicated chat and picture-sharing program that you can optionally install if you want to swap photos with your relatives, friends, and colleagues.

1 Open your Web browser (Internet Explorer, for example). In the browser's Address box, type www.hello.com to go to the Hello home page.

Download button   Download Now button

2 Click the Download or Download Now button to go to the Hello: Signup and Download page.

3 You must register in order to use Hello. Scroll down to the Sign up area. Enter a user name of your choosing, a password, and an email address at which you can be contacted. Click the Submit button to continue.

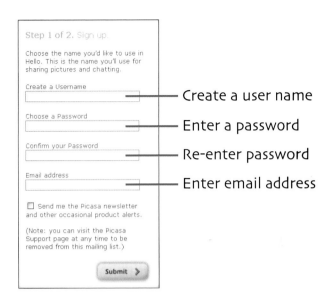

Step 1 of 2. Sign up.

Choose the name you'd like to use in Hello. This is the name you'll use for sharing pictures and chatting.

Create a Username ———————— Create a user name

Choose a Password ———————— Enter a password

Confirm your Password ———————— Re-enter password

Email address ———————— Enter email address

☐ Send me the Picasa newsletter and other occasional product alerts.

(Note: you can visit the Picasa Support page at any time to be removed from this mailing list.)

Submit >

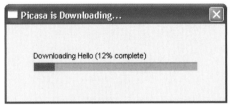

Picasa is Downloading...

Downloading Hello (12% complete)

4 If the user name is already in use, you'll be asked to select another name. Otherwise, the user name is assigned to you and the download begins.

5 The setup program launches. On the License Agreement screen, click I Agree.

6 On the Choose Install Location screen (refer to page 5), specify the hard disk folder in which to install Hello. To accept the proposed (default) folder, click Install. To specify a different folder or to create a new folder, click Browse, select a folder, and then click Install.

7 On the final screen, set any desired options and click Finish.

Run Hello when Windows Starts. Launch Hello at the start of every computing session. (This option is helpful if you're a regular Hello user. Otherwise, remove the check mark.)

Create Shortcut on Desktop. Add a Hello shortcut icon to the Desktop.

Add Shortcut to QuickLaunch. Add a Hello icon to the right of the Start button.

register a Blogger blog

If you've created—or intend to create—a Blogger-hosted blog (a journal or forum in which you can record your thoughts and exchange ideas with others), you can use a part of Hello called Bloggerbot to post photos to your blog. While this doesn't require you to install any additional software beyond Picasa and Hello, you must still register your blog as described below.

1 Open your Web browser (Internet Explorer, for example). In the browser's Address box, type www.blogger.com to go to the Blogger home page.

2 Click the Create Your Blog Now arrow. The Create Account page appears.

Create Your Blog Now

3 Enter the requested information. Be sure to review the terms of service and click the Acceptance of Terms check box. Click the Continue arrow.

Acceptance of Terms check box

installing the software

4 In the provided text boxes on the Name Blog page, name your blog and enter the URL prefix that users will type to visit the blog.

The full URL will be in the form http://prefix.blogspot.com.

Click the Continue arrow. The Choose a template page appears.

5 The layout and formatting of a Blogger blog is based on a template. To view a larger version of any template, click the template's thumbnail. Select the template whose format best suits your blog's content. Click the Continue button at the bottom of the page.

Blogger creates the new blog for you. You can now create a profile for yourself, customize the blog's appearance, and make entries in the blog.

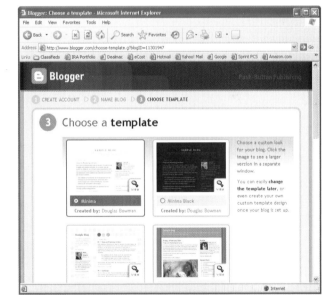

installing the software

extra bits

install Picasa 2 p. 2

- If you have an older version of Picasa on your computer, it isn't necessary to uninstall it before installing Picasa 2.

- In order to run Picasa 2, you must have Internet Explorer installed on your computer. While you don't have to make it your default browser or even use it, Internet Explorer must still be installed.

- After installing Picasa 2, you can delete the installation program.

- To get a head start on learning to use Picasa, click the Support link on Picasa's home page and then download the brief User Guide.

install Hello (optional) p. 6

- If Hello doesn't download automatically, there is a link you can click to download it manually. The manual procedure is performed in the same manner as described for downloading and installing Picasa 2.

installing the software

2. Picasa essentials

Now that you've installed Picasa 2, you're undoubtedly eager to get started. In this chapter, we'll cover the basics needed to understand and use the Picasa interface (its different display modes and the program controls you'll use to organize, view, and edit pictures), how editing works, setting program preferences, and getting help.

Initial Picture Scan

The first time you run Picasa, the Initial Picture Scan dialog box appears, explaining that Picasa is about to scan your hard disk(s) for images. The locations of all picture files found will be recorded to form your Picture Library. (These are the files you'll initially be able to work with in Picasa.)

Click a radio button to instruct Picasa to scan your whole computer or only a few common locations (depending on where you've saved your picture files), and then click Continue. When the scan finishes, you'll be ready to start working with Picasa and exploring its interface.

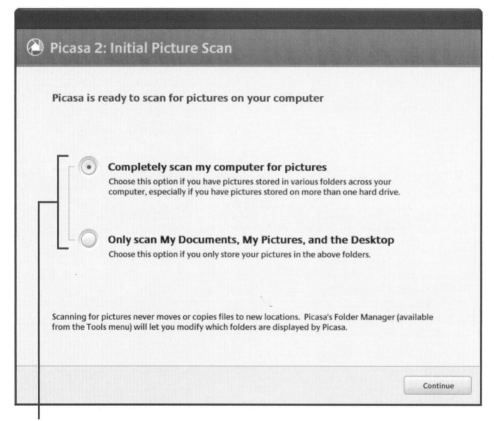

Select an option for the initial scan.

use the interface

An interface refers to the elements you interact with while using a program: menus, buttons, icons, controls, dialog boxes, and so on. Many of these elements will already be familiar to you from having used other Windows applications.

Whenever you launch Picasa, you'll first see the Picture Library (or Library). The important parts of the Picture Library interface are numbered in the screen shot below. Refer to the following pages for explanations of the parts.

Picture Library

Picture Library

1 Menus. Menus appear across the top of all Windows applications. To open a menu, click its title (such as File or View). Move the mouse down to the command you want to execute and click its name.

Some menu commands are followed by a triangle, indicating that the command has a submenu from which you must choose an option. To select such a command, move the mouse to highlight the primary command; the submenu pops out. Click the command in the submenu that you want to execute.

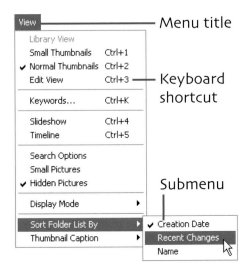

Menu title

Keyboard shortcut

Submenu

A single key (such as F2) or a key combination (such as Ctrl + 3) is listed to the right of some menu commands. These keys and combinations are referred to as keyboard shortcuts. By pressing the designated key(s), you can execute menu commands without having to open their menus.

2 Lightbox tools. As a convenience, you can execute any of these commands by clicking a button, rather than having to find them in Picasa's menus.

Folders   Collection

3 Folder List. The Folder List shows the names of all folders on your hard disks in which Picasa has found picture files. Click a folder name in the list to display the images it contains. Folders in the list are grouped within collections (folder classifications that Picasa and you create). By clicking the button to the left of a collection name, you can hide or reveal the folders in the collection. To learn more about working with collections and folders, see Chapters 3 and 4.

4 Search tool. By typing text into the Search tool's text box, you can search for matching image files and folders. Click the icon to the right of the text box to show or hide additional search options. For more information on searching, see Chapter 3.

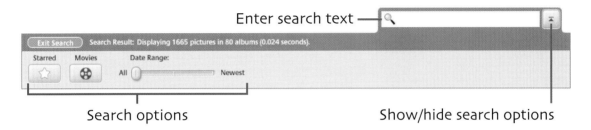

Enter search text

Search options

Show/hide search options

5 Lightbox. This refers to the right side of the Picture Library. All folders recorded by Picasa are displayed in a scrolling list—the Lightbox. The pictures in each folder are shown as miniatures called thumbnails. The effect is similar to that of a lightbox you'd use to examine photographic slides and negatives.

Double-click any thumbnail to view a full-sized version of the image. If you want to perform the same operation (such as printing) for several photos, you can select multiple thumbnails. Selected photos are shown in the Picture Tray (7).

Only one folder can be active. The active folder is shown as selected (highlighted in blue) in the Folder List, and its title bar in the Lightbox is the same color. To make a different folder active, click its name in the Folder List or click anywhere within the folder in the Lightbox.

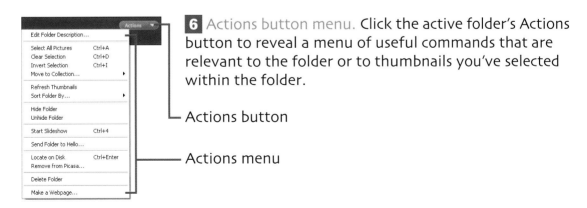

6 Actions button menu. Click the active folder's Actions button to reveal a menu of useful commands that are relevant to the folder or to thumbnails you've selected within the folder.

Actions button

Actions menu

Picture Library (cont.)

7 Picture Tray. Currently selected images appear here. You can click a button to the right to hold or clear them from the tray, send them to a printer or Hello (9), and so

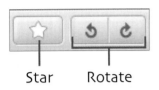

Star   Rotate

8 Star and Rotate icons. Click the Star icon to add or remove a gold star from the selected thumbnails. (Starred images are special to you in some way.) Click a Rotate icon to rotate the selected image(s) clockwise or counter-clockwise.

9 Output options. Click one of these icons to perform an output action on all images in the Picture Tray, such as printing, emailing, or exporting.

 ———— Output option icons

10 Thumbnail size slider. Drag this slider to change the size of all thumbnails in the Lightbox. (Drag to the left to make them smaller or to the right to make them larger.)

Edit View

Even at the largest thumbnail size, you won't be satisfied with looking at your favorite photos in the Lightbox. To view images at full size or larger, as well as make changes to them, you use Edit View. To open an image in Edit View, double-click its thumbnail in the Picture Library. You can also select the thumbnail and choose View > Edit View, press [Enter], or press [Ctrl][3].

The important parts of Edit View are numbered in the screen shot below. Refer to the following pages for explanations of the parts. See Chapter 5 and 6 for information about image editing.

1 Picture. The picture for the selected thumbnail appears here. You can change its size by dragging the zoom slider (7) or by clicking the first two icons (8).

Edit View (cont.)

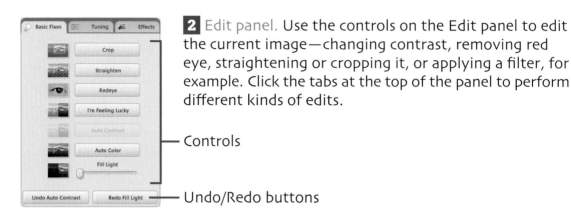

Controls

Undo/Redo buttons

2 Edit panel. Use the controls on the Edit panel to edit the current image—changing contrast, removing red eye, straightening or cropping it, or applying a filter, for example. Click the tabs at the top of the panel to perform different kinds of edits.

3 Undo/Redo buttons. Picasa has no Undo or Redo commands in its Edit menu. To undo the most recent edit for the current image, click the Undo button at the bottom of the Edit panel. To reapply an edit that you've removed by clicking Undo, click the Redo button.

Picasa supports unlimited Undos for every image. Even after quitting Picasa, you can open an image in a later session and reverse the edits by clicking Undo for each edit you want to remove.

4 Edit panel buttons. Click the buttons above the Edit panel to return to the Picture Library when you're done viewing and editing images (Back to Library), run a slide show using images from the current folder (Slideshow), or open the Help window (?).

5 Previous/Next picture. The tiny thumbnails above the open picture are images in the same folder. To view one of them, click its thumbnail. (To bring other images into view, click the left or right arrow icon.)

Scroll left Scroll right

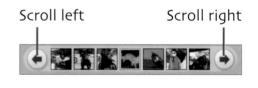

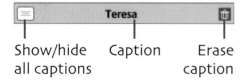

Show/hide all captions Caption Erase caption

6 Caption. To help you identify a picture, you can type a caption beneath it. To show or hide captions, click the icon to the left of the caption area. To erase a caption, click the trash icon to the right of the caption.

7 Zoom slider. To increase or decrease magnification for the current image, drag the slider to the right or left, respectively. When altering the magnification, a tiny window appears that shows the new zoom level. ——

When an image is larger (or has been zoomed larger) than will fit onscreen, you can change your view by dragging within the zoom window or by dragging the pan cursor (the hand) on the actual image.

8 Zoom size and camera information icons. There are three icons to the right of the zoom slider. The first two are for zooming, but work differently depending on the size of the picture (explained below).

Histogram & Camera Info.

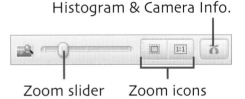

Zoom slider   Zoom icons

When you first open a picture in Edit View or click Fit (the first icon), the picture is displayed at its actual size if it is smaller than the display area; if it is larger, it is reduced to completely fill the display area's width, height, or both. Clicking Actual Size (the second icon) sets magnification at 100 percent for pictures that are larger than will fit in the display area; small pictures that will not fill the display area are zoomed to 200 percent.

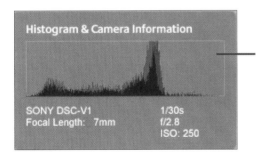

Click Histogram & Camera Information (the third icon) to display a color dispersion histogram and any EXIF camera data stored with the photo. The information box remains onscreen when you switch from image to image. However, if you zoom the image, the box is replaced by the Zoomed to box (see Point 7 above).

about editing in Picasa

Picasa is different from other image-editing applications. Edits made in Picasa do not alter the original image file. If you open the file in another program, you'll see the original, unedited picture. Picasa merely tracks edits, enabling you to view and print pictures in it as though the edits had actually changed the file.

When you need to move pictures to another computer or edit them in other programs, Picasa has procedures for saving and exporting your edited images to new files that reflect your edits (see Chapter 9). And when you email pictures directly from Picasa (see Chapter 7), the conversion is automatically performed for you.

One advantage of the way Picasa handles edits is that you can step back through them, removing their effects in reverse order (from most recent to oldest edit) at any time. Open the edited image in Edit View and click the Undo button once for each edit you want to remove. The button's label changes to reflect the specific edit you will Undo.

After you Undo an edit, the Redo button also becomes available. You can click it to reapply the edit you removed.

—— Undo and Redo buttons

General options

Like other programs, you can customize certain Picasa features and tools to suit the way you work. Choose Tools > Options. In the Options dialog box that appears, you can set four classes of preferences: General, E-Mail, File Types, and Slideshow. After making the desired changes, click Apply and then OK. In the following pages, I'll discuss these options—starting with the General options.

General options

Check for online updates every time I start Picasa. Normally, you'll want this option enabled. If Picasa/Google issues a new version or update, you will automatically be notified. If you remove the check mark, you can periodically check for updates by choosing Help > Check for Updates Online.

Automatically detect media. Unnecessary if you're running Windows XP, this option can be useful if Windows doesn't automatically detect the presence of a newly connected digital camera or a card reader into which you've inserted a memory card.

Automatically detect duplicate files while importing. If you have pictures stored in multiple locations (computers, memory cards, or CDs/DVDs), this function will prevent you from importing images that are already on the target computer.

Use special effects in user interface. When enabled, Picasa uses a special effect, such as a fade, when moving between program components (returning from Edit View to the Picture Library, for instance). If disabled, the new screen simply replaces the previous screen.

General options (cont.)

Show tooltips. A tooltip is explanatory text that pops up when you rest the cursor over some interface elements, such as buttons, icons, and controls. Until you're thoroughly familiar with Picasa, you'll probably want to leave this option checked.

Single-click to exit Edit View. In addition to clicking the Back To Library button, you can also exit Edit View by clicking the current picture. When this option is checked, a single click is required; when unchecked, you must double click the picture.

Printer Quality Setting and Printer Resampler Quality. Choices here represent your default print quality settings. You can override these settings by clicking the Printer Setup button. See Chapter 7 for information about printing.

Save Imported Pictures In. When importing images from a digital camera, CD, or other source, this is the default folder into which the pictures will be copied. To specify a different folder, click Browse, select a folder in the Browse for Folder dialog box, and click OK. See Chapter 4 for details on importing images.

As necessary, open folders until you locate the one you want. Highlight the folder and click OK.

E-Mail options

Settings on the E-Mail tab of the Options dialog box determine what happens when you email pictures from within Picasa.

E-Mail Program. Select the email program you'll normally use when emailing photos from Picasa. When you choose File > E-Mail or click the Email button at the bottom of the Picasa window, a new email message will be created in the specified email program. All currently selected pictures will be added as message attachments. You can select your default email program, Picasa Mail (if you're a registered Hello user), or Gmail (Google email).

If you want the option to pick a different program whenever you execute the E-Mail command, click the Let me choose each time I send pictures check box.

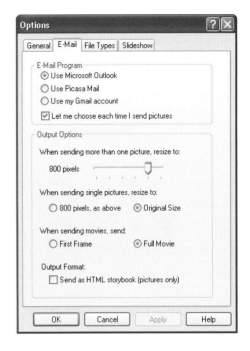

E-Mail options

Settings in the Output Options section determine whether pictures will be resized when sent as attachments, as well as their output format.

When sending more than one picture, resize to. Drag the slider to set the maximum image size when sending multiple attachments in a message. Only pictures larger than the specified size will be resized.

When sending single pictures, resize to. Select either the size specified for multiple pictures (the previous option) or Original Size (to prevent any single picture attachment from being resized.)

When sending movies, send. You can send the First Frame (as a single image) or the Full Movie. (However, since the point of emailing a movie is to enable the recipient to view it, you'll normally want to send the full movie.)

E-Mail options (cont.)

Send as HTML storybook (pictures only). Rather than sending pictures as attachments, you can check this option to send them embedded in the message in "storybook" format. This is an excellent option if you regularly email photos to friends and relatives who have difficulty dealing with attachments. You're free to edit any text (such as the image labels) in the Picasa-generated messages.

Note: For this option to work, you must use a standard email program—not Picasa Mail or Gmail—and set that program's default message format to HTML.

This is an example of a message with photos sent as an HTML storybook.

Editable text

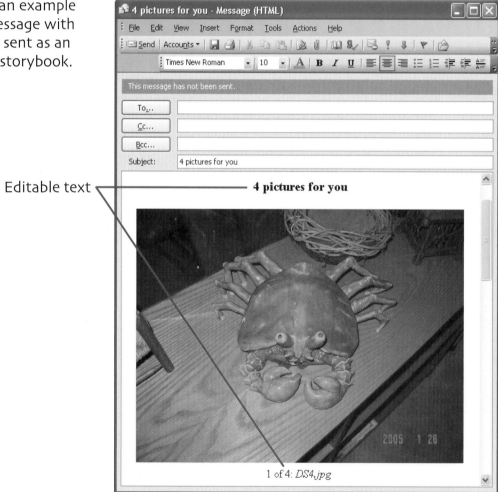

File Types options

Click check boxes on this tab to specify the file types that Picasa will track and display.

Note: On its first scan (see page 12), Picasa skips GIF (Graphics Interchange Format) and PNG (Portable Network Graphics) files. Both file formats are used for Web graphics. Of the two, GIF files are more common, though. To instruct Picasa to track these file types, click their check boxes.

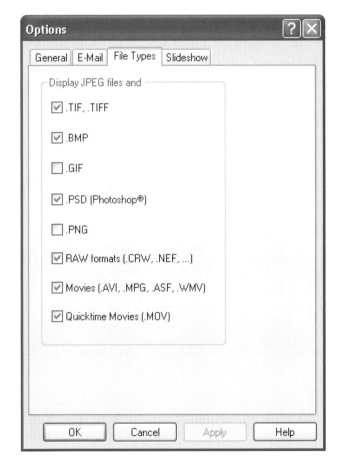

File Types options

Make any desired changes to the list of tracked file types by adding and/or clearing check marks. When you click OK to close the dialog box, Picasa will update the Picture Library accordingly.

Slideshow options

Options on this tab determine some key behaviors of Picasa slide shows (whether generated with the View > Slideshow or View > Timeline command).

Loop slideshow. Slide shows normally display each image in the selected folder or label only once. Check this option to make a show loop repeatedly through the pictures until it's manually halted.

Play MP3 tracks during slideshow. When checked, slide shows will be accompanied by MP3 music files found in the folder specified on this tab. To select a different folder, click the Browse button.

Do full-resolution slideshow. Check this option for higher quality slide shows. Remove the check mark if you have an older or less capable computer.

Slideshow options

Picasa essentials

get help with Picasa

Picasa provides many sources of support that you can consult to learn about program features and resolve problems, including a brief manual, built-in Help, an online knowledge base, and user forums. These help sources (or Web links to them) are all accessible from the Help menu.

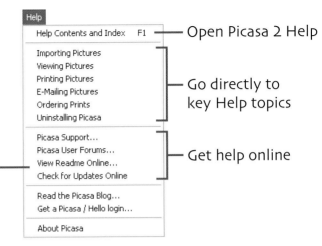

Open Picasa 2 Help

Go directly to key Help topics

Get help online

To open Picasa 2 Help, choose Help > Help Contents and Index, press F1, or choose a specific topic from the Help menu. You can also click a ? button in a Picasa dialog box or another part of the interface. To view Help topics on the Contents tab, refer to the figure below.

Contents tab

Topic title

Select a topic in the Contents list

Click underlined text to switch topics or read related text

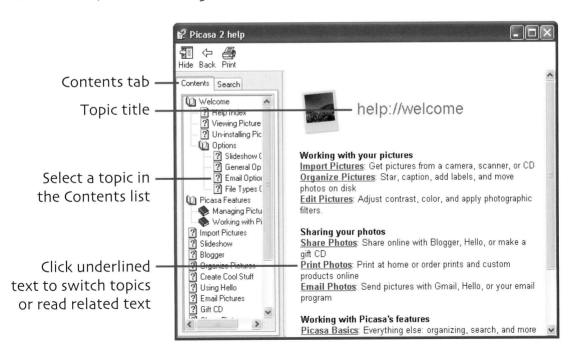

get help with Picasa (cont.)

In addition to browsing topics on the Contents tab, you can click the Search tab to search Picasa 2 Help for topics that contain certain text.

1 Enter search text in the box and then click the List Topics button. Relevant topics appear in a list below.

2 Select a topic and click Display to view the selected Help text.

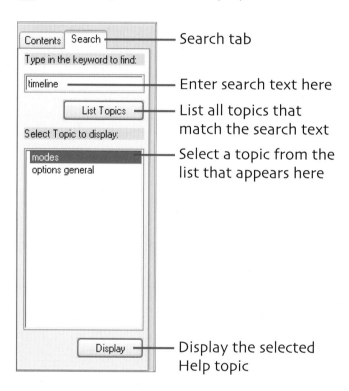

— Search tab

— Enter search text here

— List all topics that match the search text

— Select a topic from the list that appears here

— Display the selected Help topic

extra bits

Initial Picture Scan p. 12

- The Initial Picture Scan option you pick may depend on whether or not you followed Windows conventions by storing images in the folders that Windows provides for such files.

  As a long-time PC user, I already had other folders for image files, organized in a way that made sense to me. Thus, scanning the entire computer was the best choice for me.

- Regardless of the scan option you select, you can use the Folder Manager to add or remove folders by following the instructions in Chapter 4.

use the interface p. 13

- To change the order of folders in the collections, you can choose a command from the View > Sort Folder List By submenu.

- While the program areas in which you'll spend most of your time working are the Picture Library and Edit View, you'll occasionally run slide shows, too. See Chapter 3 for instructions on interacting with and controlling slide shows.

Picture Library p. 14

- To see a full-screen version of a selected thumbnail, press Ctrl Alt. When you release the keys, you'll return to the Picture Library. You can also do this in Edit View.

- You can open a pop-up menu of relevant commands by right-clicking any blank spot in the Lightbox, a thumbnail, or a folder or collection name in the Folder List. You can also right-click the current image in Edit View.

Edit View p. 17

- Other ways to exit from Edit View and return to the Picture Library include double-clicking the current picture or pressing Esc.

E-Mail Options p. 23

- When emailing from Picasa, all image attachments are converted to JPEG files. If you want to send an image that's in a different file format (such as TIFF) without losing that format, don't email it from within Picasa. Instead, open your email program and attach the file to a new message.

extra bits

File Types Options p. 25

- If you aren't sure if adding GIF and PNG file tracking is worthwhile, try it. If the Picture Library is suddenly littered with unwanted files, return to this Options tab and remove the two check marks.

Slideshow Options p. 26

- Unlike most options, you may want to reset Slideshow Options before each new show, depending on the effect you want to achieve.

- When playing MP3 music with a slide show, you have no control over which files are played. If Picasa finds multiple MP3s in the specified folder, it plays them in alphabetical order. To force one particular MP3 to play, rename it so it comes first in the folder or move it into a folder in which it is the only MP3 file.

get help with Picasa p. 27

- To get a copy of the Picasa 2 User Guide, choose Help > Picasa Support and click the link on the Web page that appears. A PDF (Adobe Acrobat) version of the manual will download.

3. viewing photos

While organizing and sharing your photos are both important, it's likely that the first thing you'll want to do with Picasa is learn the different ways you can view your pictures. Picasa provides several different viewing options, as well as tools to find precisely the images you want to view.

In this chapter, you'll learn to work in the Picture Library—setting thumbnail properties, sorting the Folder List and individual folders, searching for images, and selecting files. You'll also find out how to open images for viewing, change the display mode, run a slide show, and use Timeline view to look at photos in date sequence.

Chapter 4 describes Picasa tools for better organizing your image files, making them easier for you to find. Because organizing and viewing go hand-in-hand, you should read these two chapters together.

view a picture

You can open and view any picture that is stored in the Picture Library.

1 Find the thumbnail of the image you want to view. To bring its thumbnail into view, you can click the scroll arrows on the right side of the Lightbox or click its folder name in the Folder List. (If the folder is hidden within a collapsed collection, click the triangle button to the left of the collection name to expand the collection.)

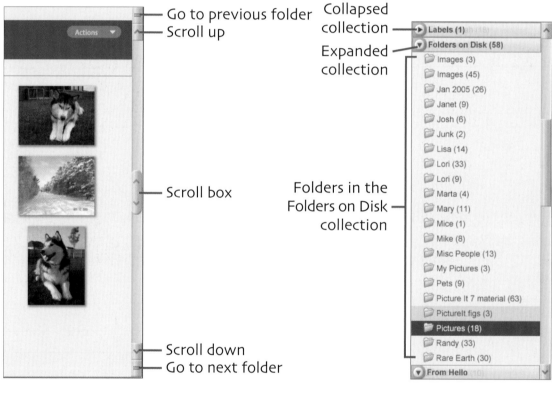

Go to previous folder
Scroll up
Collapsed collection
Expanded collection
Scroll box
Folders in the Folders on Disk collection
Scroll down
Go to next folder

Scroll bar

Folder List

2 To view the image in Edit View, double-click its thumbnail. (Or select the thumbnail and then choose Picture > View and Edit, press [Enter], or press [Ctrl][3]).

viewing photos

3 As explained in Chapter 2, you can drag the zoom slider to change the magnification, or click an icon beneath the picture to resize the image to fit the window or display it at full size. When an image is larger than will fit in the window, you can click and drag the hand cursor to see other areas of the image.

To view other images in the same folder, click a thumbnail above the picture or one of the arrow icons. When you're done, click the Back To Library button or press Esc.

Back To Library   Previous image   Next image

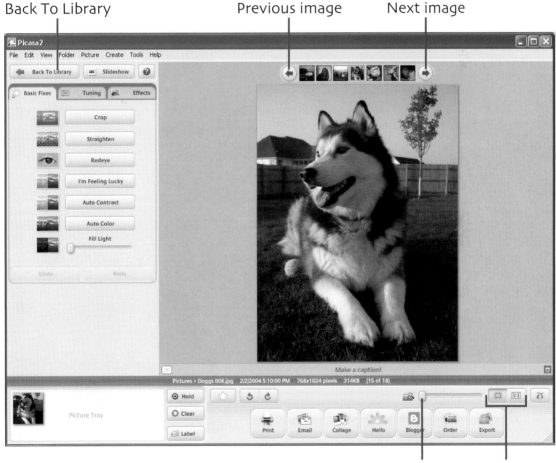

Zoom slider   Resize

work with thumbnails

While working in the Picture Library, there are many commands and program controls to make it easier to find and select the specific images you want to edit, display as a slide show, or print. In this and the following sections, you'll learn about them, starting with procedures for working with thumbnails.

Adjust thumbnail sizes. Whenever you like, you can change the size of the thumbnails in the Lightbox. You can make them very small to see every image in a packed folder or very large to get better idea of image quality and subject matter. To change thumbnail size, drag the slider beneath the Lightbox, choose a View menu command, or press a ⌈Ctrl⌉ key shortcut.

Smaller   Larger

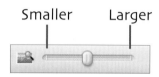

Drag this slider to set thumbnail size.

To quickly set thumbnails to the smallest or normal size, choose a View command or press ⌈Ctrl⌉⌈1⌉ (small) or ⌈Ctrl⌉⌈2⌉ (normal).

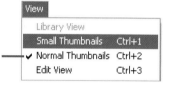

Set thumbnail captions. Every thumbnail can optionally be labeled to make it easier for you to tell one picture from another. Choose a labeling option from the View > Thumbnail Caption submenu.

Refresh thumbnails. If you think the thumbnails in the current folder don't accurately show recent edits, newly added images, or deleted files, choose Folder > Refresh Thumbnails. (This command can also be chosen from the folder's Actions button menu.)

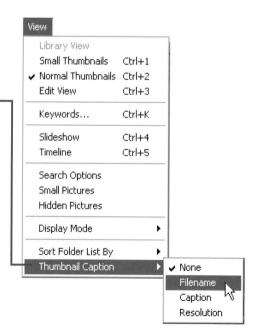

Picasa checks for file changes and adjusts the folder's thumbnails as necessary—adding ones for new files, removing those of deleted files, and modifying thumbnail images to reflect recent edits.

sort folders and files

Picasa provides two sorting commands that you can use as needed to make it simpler to find pictures. First, you can set a sort order for folders in the Folder List. Second, you can specify a sort order for the images within any folder.

Sort folders in the Folder List. To sort the folders within each collection, choose Creation Date, Recent Changes, or Name from the View > Sort Folder List By submenu.

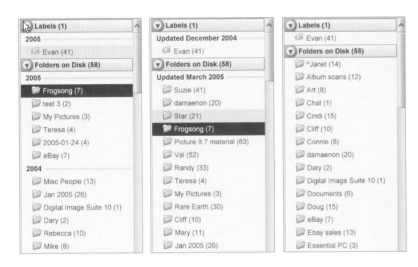

Creation Date   Recent Changes   Name

These are examples of the three folder sort options. Note that each collection is sorted separately.

Sort within a folder. Choose a command from the Folder > Sort By submenu (Name, Date, or Size) to set an order for the images in the current folder. (You can also choose a Sort Folder By command from the Actions button menu.) Every folder can have a different sort order.

Folder sorted by Name (filename)

set display options

By making menu choices, you can set display settings that determine how the interface and images look, as well as which thumbnails are visible.

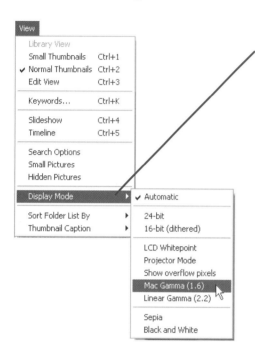

Set the display mode. By choosing a command from the View > Display Mode submenu, you can force a specific display setting. Normally, this should be left as Automatic (the default choice). The setting affects the entire interface, including the Picture Library and images opened for editing or viewing.

Use a setting from the third group when you need to adjust pictures for a particular output medium, such as display on a Mac.

Choose a display mode from the last group to get a quick idea of how pictures will look if the sepia or black-and-white filter is applied to them (described in Chapter 6).

View small or hidden pictures. Normally, two classes of images are stored in the Picture Library but not displayed as thumbnails: tiny pictures (such as Web graphics) and pictures that you deliberately hid using the Picture > Hide command. You can reveal these image groups by choosing View > Small Pictures or View > Hidden Pictures. (When the command is checked in the menu, the chosen image class is visible. Choose the same command again to reverse the setting.)

Note: Unlike hidden folders, hidden images aren't password-protected (see Chapter 4).

Hidden pictures

search for pictures

In addition to browsing through folders, you can use Picasa's Search feature to quickly find specific images in the Picture Library.

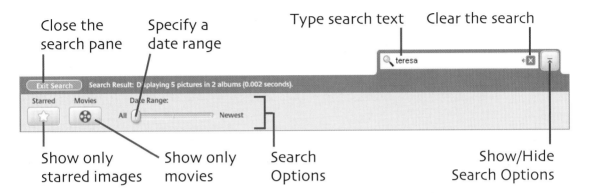

Close the search pane · Specify a date range · Type search text · Clear the search

Show only starred images · Show only movies · Search Options · Show/Hide Search Options

1 Type search text in the box at the top of the search pane. As you type, Picasa automatically hides all images that do not match the search text.

When determining which images match, Picasa considers all text associated with each picture: filename; caption; keywords; folder, label, and collection name; date; colors used; and camera maker and EXIF data.

2 Optional: For greater precision in a search (showing only starred images that match the search text, for instance), display the bottom part of the search pane. Click the Show/Hide Search Options icon or choose View > Search Options.

To show only matching images that are also starred and/or movies, click the appropriate icon(s). To restrict the date range of matching images, drag the Date Range slider.

3 Select or open images as you normally do.

4 To return to viewing the entire Picture Library or to conduct a new search, click the Clear icon to the right of the search text. Or you can clear the search and simultaneously close the lower part of the search pane by clicking the Exit Search button.

select multiple images

While you can only open one file at a time for viewing or editing, many Picasa procedures work with multiple images. Most of the multi-image selection techniques described below can be used in combination with one another.

Select a single image by clicking its thumbnail, placing the image in the Picture Tray. If you click another thumbnail, it replaces the one in the Picture Tray.

Select any contiguous group of images in a folder or label by (Shift)-clicking the first and last thumbnails in the group or by dragging a selection rectangle around the group.

Select non-contiguous images in a folder or label by (Ctrl)-clicking each one.

Select starred images in the current folder or label by clicking the Starred text beneath the folder/label name or by choosing Edit > Select Starred.

Select every image in a folder or label other than the currently selected ones (inverting the selection) by choosing Edit > Invert Selection ((Ctrl)(I)).

Select all images in the current folder or label by clicking the All text beneath the folder/label name or by choosing Edit > Select All ((Ctrl)(A)).

Combine multiple selections by clicking the Hold button beside the Picture Tray after adding each group. When you click Hold, images currently in the Picture Tray are marked with a green target symbol. You can then freely add other images without worrying about the current ones being cleared. You must use this technique to select images from multiple folders.

Hold marker

Hold selections

Clear selections

To deselect all selected images in the current folder or label, click the None text beneath the folder/label, click a blank area in the Lightbox, or choose Edit > Clear Selection ((Ctrl)(D)). To clear all images from the Picture Tray, click the Clear button and click Yes in the Confirm dialog box that appears.

run a slide show

Using the Slideshow feature, you can run a full-screen show of all pictures in any folder or label. Controls are available at the bottom of the show, enabling you to set options, skip forward or backward, and rotate individual images, for example. (Some display and play options are governed by settings in the Options dialog box. See Chapter 2 for details.)

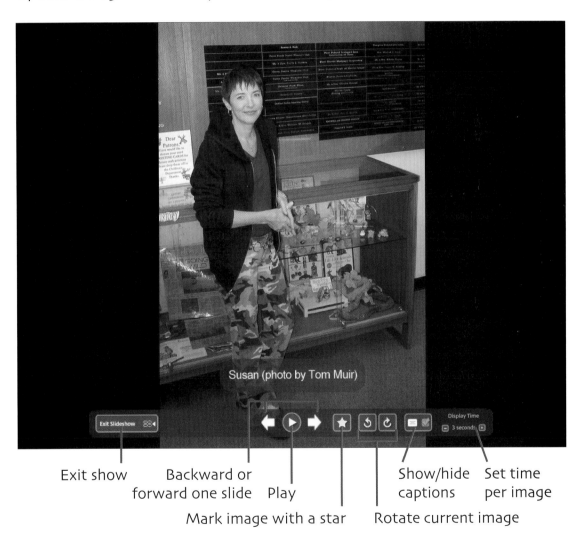

Susan (photo by Tom Muir)

Exit show | Backward or forward one slide | Play | Mark image with a star | Rotate current image | Show/hide captions | Set time per image

run a slide show (cont.)

1 Select the folder or label that you want to display as a slide show. (If you select a specific thumbnail, the show will start with that image. Otherwise, it will start with the first image in the folder or label.)

2 Click the Slideshow button above the Picture Library or the Edit pane, choose View > Slideshow, or press (Ctrl)(4). The slide show begins.

3 Optional: If you want to interrupt the show or change some settings, move the mouse. A settings control strip appears at the bottom of the screen.

By clicking the strip's icons (from left to right), you can end the slide show, move back to the previous slide, continue playing, skip forward to the next slide, add or remove a star from the current slide, rotate the current slide counterclockwise or clockwise, show or hide captions for all slides, or change the duration that each slide stays onscreen. When you're done making changes, click the Play button or press (Spacebar) to resume the slide show.

Note: Changes to an image's rotation or star setting are retained after you exit the slide show.

use Timeline view

Think of the Timeline feature as a special interface for slide shows. All folders and labels are presented in the timeline in date order. You use the timeline to select the folder or label on which to base a slide show. After the show, you can exit to the Picture Library or select another folder in the timeline to view.

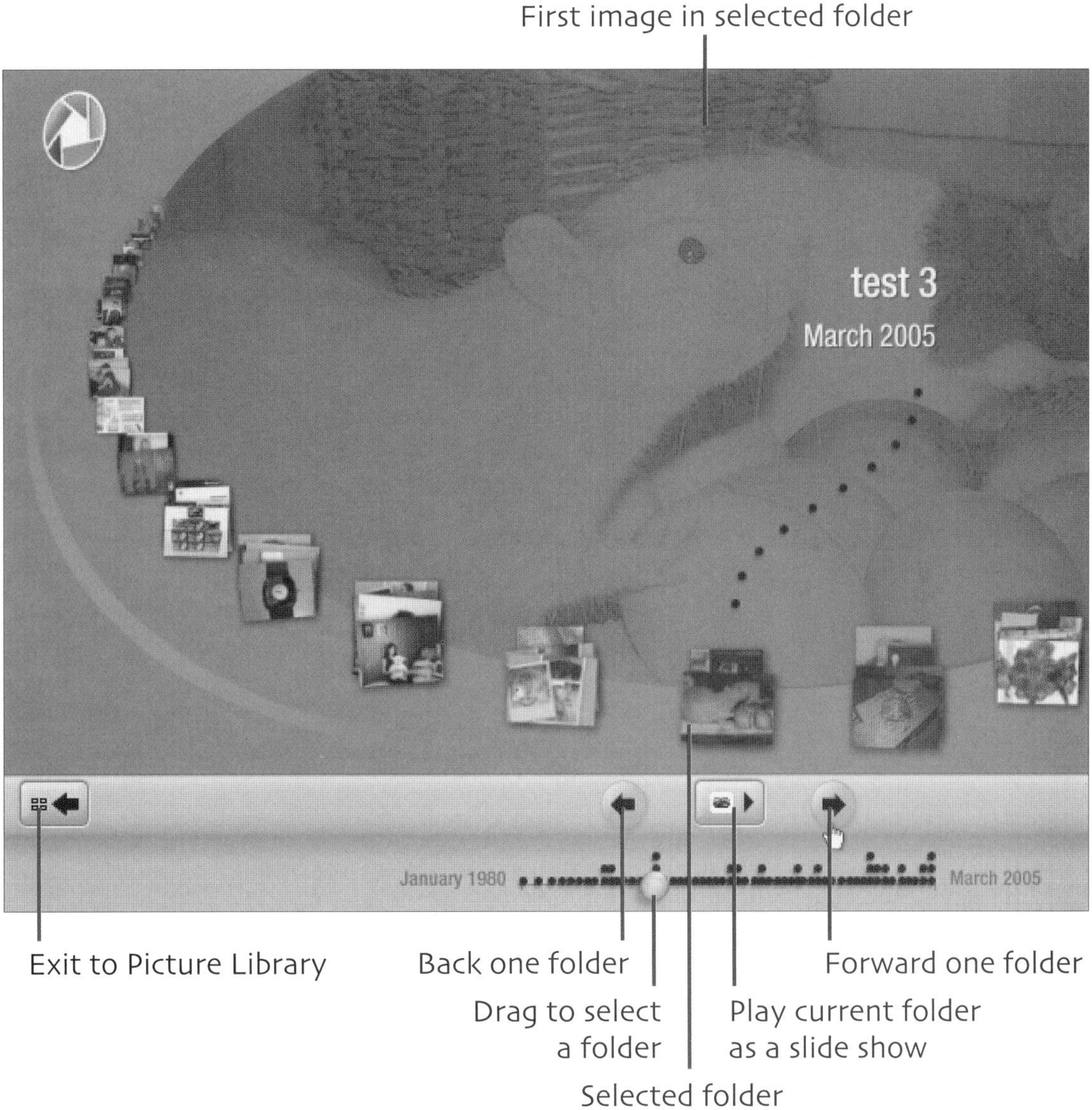

First image in selected folder

test 3
March 2005

January 1980   March 2005

Exit to Picture Library   Back one folder   Forward one folder

Drag to select   Play current folder
a folder   as a slide show

Selected folder

use Timeline view (cont.)

1 Click the Timeline button above the Picture Library, choose View > Timeline, or press (Ctrl)(5). The Timeline interface appears (see previous page).

2 Using the controls at the bottom of the Timeline interface, select a folder or label to view. Click the Play button to begin the slide show.

Play

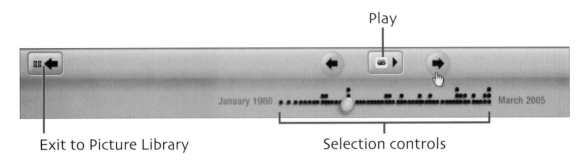

Exit to Picture Library   Selection controls

3 Optional: While viewing a show, you can change its settings. Move the mouse to display the control strip at the bottom of the screen and make any necessary changes (see instructions for "Run a slide show"). Click the Play button or press (Spacebar) to resume the show.

To halt the current show and select a different folder, click the Timeline button on the control strip. To halt the show and return directly to the Picture Library, click the Exit Slideshow button.

Return to Picture   Return to Timeline
Library   interface

4 After each slide show, the Timeline interface reappears. Select a new folder and repeat Steps 2 and 3, or click the Exit button to return to the Picture Library.

extra bits

view a picture p. 32

- As you'll learn in Chapters 5 and 6, you can also edit the current picture in Edit View.

- You can display a color dispersion histogram and any EXIF camera data that's stored with an image by clicking the Show/Hide Histogram & Camera Information icon (the beanie beneath the picture).

- You can also open any selected picture in another program, if you like. You might want to do some advanced editing in a program that has different features than Picasa, for example.

  To open all selected images in your default editor/viewer (Windows Picture and Fax Viewer, for example), choose File > Open File(s) in an Editor. To use a particular editor, right-click a selected image and choose Open With, followed by the program name. (Recently used editors are listed in the Open With submenu.)

- To view a picture's EXIF camera data, select its thumbnail and choose Picture > Properties or press Alt Enter.

set display options p. 36

- To prevent certain folders or files from cluttering up the Library or to prevent them from being seen by others, you can hide them, as explained in Chapter 4.

search for pictures p. 37

- You don't always need to enter search text. You can filter the Picture Library to show only starred files, movies, or a date range by using any combination of those three search controls.

run a slide show p. 39

- Because you can alter a photo's star setting during a slide show (while viewing full-screen images), you may find it more convenient to do so than while working in the Picture Library.

run a Timeline show p. 41

- To immediately end a show or exit from the Timeline interface, you can also press Esc.

4. organizing pictures

The first time you launch Picasa, it automatically scans all hard disks for image files. The names of folders that contain one or more image files are automatically added to Picasa's Folder List, enabling you to view and edit the files. In this chapter, you'll learn about Picasa procedures and techniques for organizing images—making them easier to find when performing searches and arranging them to better suit the way you work and think.

Folder List   File

Collection

Folders

Picture Tray

work with collections

You use collections to organize folders in Picasa. Think of a collection as a master folder—a container of other folders that share something in common, such as all family photos or pictures downloaded from the Web, for example. Unlike the folders in the Folder List (which represent actual directories on your hard disks), a collection exists only in Picasa.

When you run Picasa for the first time, it automatically creates two collections: Folders on Disk and Other Stuff. Picasa puts all folders that contain large images into the Folders on Disk collection; folders with smaller files are placed in the Other Stuff collection. Certain actions automatically create additional collections. For example, receiving files from Hello (Chapter 10) creates a From Hello collection, exporting images to a folder (Chapter 9) creates an Exported Pictures collection, and defining your first label creates a Labels collection.

Create collections. You can also create your own collections to organize folders.

1 Every collection must contain at least one folder. In the Folder List, right-click any folder you want to include in the new collection. Choose Move to Collection > New Collection from the menu that appears.

2 In the Add New Collection dialog box, name the new collection and click OK.

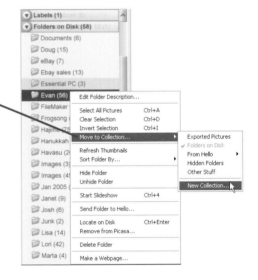

3 The new collection appears in the Folder List, alphabetized by its name.

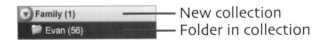

New collection — Family (1)
Folder in collection — Evan (56)

organizing pictures

Move a folder to a different collection. Each folder can be in only one collection. To make folders as easy as possible for you to find, it's important that every one be in the most appropriate collection. You may want to reclassify some of the folders that were assigned to the Folders on Disk and Other Stuff collections, for example. You'll also want to do some reorganizing when you create new collections or add folders to the Picture Library.

1 In the Folder List, right-click the folder you want to move.

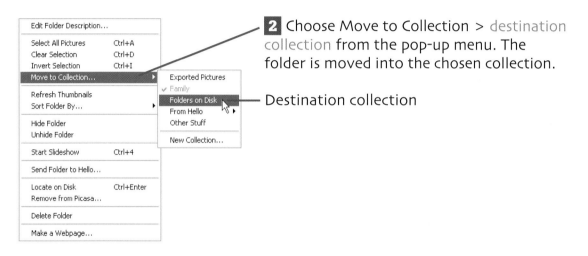

2 Choose Move to Collection > destination collection from the pop-up menu. The folder is moved into the chosen collection.

Destination collection

Rename a collection. While the names of automatically generated collections can't be changed, you can freely rename any collection you've created.

1 Right-click the collection name in the Folder List, and choose Rename Collection from the pop-up menu that appears.

2 Edit the name in the Rename Collection dialog box, and then click OK.

Collection name in Folder List

work with collections (cont.)

Password-protect a collection. You can assign a password to a collection to prevent others from seeing the folders and images within it. Whenever someone tries to view the collection by opening it in the Folder List, a Password Entry dialog box is presented.

1 Right-click the collection name in the Folder List. Choose Add/Change a password from the pop-up menu that appears (see previous page).

2 In the Password Entry dialog box, type the password you'd like to assign to the collection and click OK. Type the password again in the Password Verify dialog box and click OK. The password is now associated with the collection.

Collapsing the collection in the Folder List protects it. To do so, click the triangle button beside the collection's name. The next time you want to view the collection, click the triangle button again and supply the requested password.

To change a password, open the protected collection by supplying the current password. Right-click the collection name in the Folder List, and then choose Add/Change a password. Enter the new password and confirm it (see Step 2).

To remove password protection from a collection, open the protected collection by supplying the password. Then right-click the collection name in the Folder List, and choose Add/Change a password. Instead of entering a password, leave the dialog box blank and press Enter (or click OK).

Remove a collection. You can eliminate collections that are no longer needed. Right-click the collection name in the Folder List, and choose Remove Collection from the pop-up menu that appears (see previous page). Click Yes in the Confirm dialog box. Any folders contained within the removed collection are moved to the Other Stuff collection. You can move those folders to a different collection by following the instructions on the previous page.

Confirm dialog box

work with labels

Just as collections are used to organize folders with common content, you can create labels (special Picasa-only folders) to group similar files—regardless of their location on disk. Although a folder can be in only one collection, an image file can be in as many label folders as you want. Adding a picture to a label doesn't move it from its folder on your hard disk. Files in a label are simply shortcuts to the originals rather than the actual files. As such, removing a file from a label doesn't delete it.

Create labels. You can create as many labels as you like. After creating the first label, Picasa creates a Labels collection in which all labels are stored.

1 Select the images for this label, adding them to the Picture Tray. (To include images from multiple folders, click Hold after selecting images from each folder.)

Picture Tray — | — Hold selected pictures

— Label button

2 Choose File > New Label, click the Label button (beside the Picture Tray) and choose New Label, or press [Ctrl][N]. The Label Properties dialog box appears. ——

3 Type a name and select a date for the new label. (The date can be when the label was created or when the pictures were shot, for example.) If you like, you can enter information regarding where the pictures were taken and a description.

4 Click OK to add the new label to the Labels collection.

Labels collection —— Labels (1)

New label —— Evan (33)

work with labels (cont.)

Add pictures to a label. To add new pictures to an existing label, select their thumbnails, click the Label button, and choose the label from the pop-up menu.

You can also add a picture to an existing label by right-clicking its thumbnail in the Library or its picture in Edit View. Then choose a label from the pop-up menu that appears.

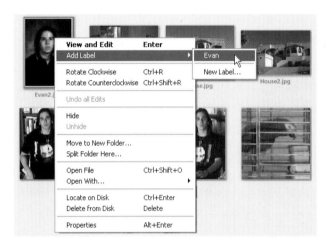

You can right-click a thumbnail...   ...or right-click an open picture.

Remove pictures from a label. If you later want to remove a picture from a label, select the label in the Folders List. Then select the image's thumbnail, and choose File > Remove from Label or press [Del]. Confirm the Deletion by clicking Yes in the dialog box that appears. Note that removing an image from a label does not delete its file; it just breaks the association between it and the label.

Delete a label. To delete a label you no longer need, select the label in the Folders List. Choose Label > Delete or press [Del]. Confirm the Deletion by clicking Yes in the dialog box that appears. (Note that deleting a label does not delete its files or remove them from their normal Picasa or Windows folders.)

work with folders

All image files are organized in folders, and every folder corresponds to an actual folder on disk. Actions that you perform on folders within Picasa affect the folders on disk, too. As such, you can modify any image folder and its contents from within Picasa or by doing so in Windows.

Most folder commands can be chosen from a menu, by clicking the folder's Actions button, or by right-clicking the folder name in the Folder List (or almost anywhere else within the folder's area in the Lightbox).

Actions drop-down menu

Folder menu   Actions button   Right-clicking within a folder

Change folder properties. Choose Folder > Edit Description (or the Edit Folder Description command). In the Folder Properties dialog box, you can alter the folder name and date, describe where the folder's photos were taken, or add a caption. Click OK to set the new folder properties.

Changes made in the Folder Properties dialog box appear in Picasa in the blue green bar above the folder's image thumbnails.

work with folders (cont.)

Split a folder. Use the Split Folder Here command to split a folder's pictures into two folders, starting at the selected picture in the current sort order.

1 Choose a command from the Folder > Sort By submenu to arrange the folder's images in the desired order.

2 Right-click the thumbnail where you want to divide the folder's images. Then choose Split Folder Here from the pop-up menu that appears.

Split folder starting with this image ——

3 A Folder Properties dialog box appears (see page 51). Name the new folder, enter other information as desired, and click OK. Starting with the selected thumbnail, the image and all those following it are moved to the new folder.

Open a folder on disk. To see a folder's contents (including files other than images, you can open it using several Picasa procedures. The simplest is to click the folder icon in the blue green bar above the folder's thumbnails.

You can also select the folder in the Folder List and press (Ctrl)(Enter) (or choose Folder > Locate on Disk). This command can also be chosen by right-clicking anywhere within the folder or from the Actions button's drop-down menu.

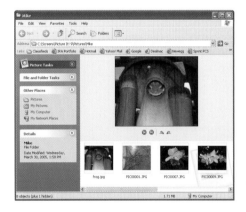

The Locate on Disk command opens the selected Windows folder.

organizing pictures

Delete a folder. This is Picasa's most dangerous command. Use it to delete a folder and its contents from your hard disk. Because a folder can contain files in addition to the graphics shown in Picasa, you should always inspect a folder's contents before deleting it. See "Open a folder on disk" on the previous page for instructions.

1 Select the folder name in the folder list and choose Folder > Delete.

You can also choose the Delete Folder command from the Actions button menu or when right-clicking the folder name/area.

2 Click Yes in the Confirm dialog box that appears. The folder and its files are moved to the Recycle Bin.

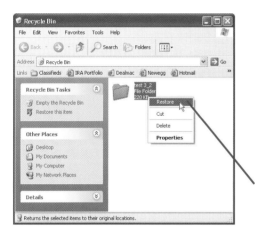

If you act quickly, you can recover a deleted folder. Open the Recycle Bin, right-click the folder, and choose Restore from the pop-up menu. Be sure to do this before you empty the Recycle Bin!

Remove a folder from Picasa. There are many folders Picasa tracks automatically that you probably don't want cluttering up the Folder List. Examples include folders containing only program startup screens or sample images. You can remove these folders from Picasa without affecting them on disk.

1 Select the folder, making it active. Then choose the Remove from Picasa command from the Folder, Actions button, or right-click menu. The Folder Manager appears (see page 55) with the selected folder highlighted.

2 Click the Remove from Picasa radio button, and then click OK. The folder is removed from the Folder List.

work with folders (cont.)

Hide folders. If there are folders you want to view but keep secret from others, you can hide them. This is accomplished by creating a password-protected Hidden Folders collection.

1 Select the first folder you want to hide. Choose Folder > Hide, choose Hide Folder from the Actions button drop-down menu, or right-click the folder name and choose Hide Folder.

2 The Add Password dialog box appears. Click Yes to create a password for the Hidden Folders collection.

Add Password

The "Hidden Folders" collection is not currently password protected. Would you like to add a password now?

☐ Do not ask me again.   [Yes]   [No]

Password Entry ☒

Please enter a password to use for this collection

✱✱✱✱✱

[OK]   [Cancel]   [Help]

3 Type the password in the Password Entry dialog box and click OK. Type the password again in the Password Verify dialog box, and then click OK.

The Hidden Folders collection is created in the Folder List. Each time you attempt to open/expand the collection, you'll be prompted to enter the password.

To ensure that the Hidden Folders collection is locked at the end of a session, collapse it, select a folder in a different collection, and then quit Picasa.

To add another folder to the Hidden Folders collection, select the folder and then choose Folder > Hide, choose Hide Folder from the Actions button drop-down menu, or right-click the folder name and choose Hide Folder.

To remove a folder from the Hidden Folders collection, expand the collection, select the folder name, and choose Folder > Unhide. The folder is restored to its previous collection.

Use the Folder Manager. You use the Folder Manager to determine the changes—if any—Picasa tracks for each folder on your hard disk(s). For each folder, you can tell Picasa to Remove from Picasa (ignore the folder, as explained earlier in the chapter), Watch for Changes (automatically track all changes), or Scan Once (ignoring future changes to the folder's image files).

To open the Folder Manager, choose Tools > Folder Manager. Select the folder and then click a radio button to indicate how Picasa will track changes to the folder's contents. Click OK to save all changed folder settings.

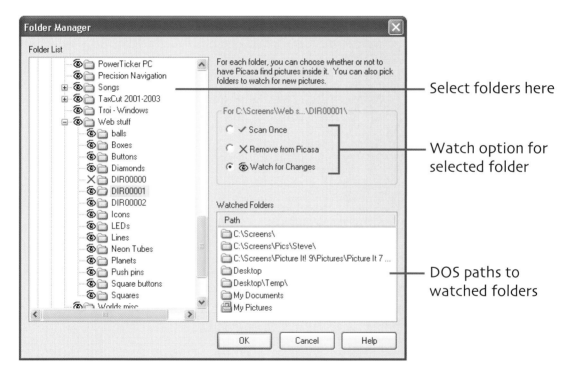

Select folders here

Watch option for selected folder

DOS paths to watched folders

Note: If you make major changes to the Folder Manager settings, Picasa may wait to update its database until the next time you launch the program.

work with files

Using Picasa's file-related commands and procedures, you can move files to a different folder; rename, delete, or hide files; assign keywords, captions, or a star to a file; and locate files on disk. As is the case with folder commands, certain file commands also affect the actual files on disk.

Move pictures to another folder. To move pictures from one Picasa folder to another, you use drag-and-drop; that is, you select file thumbnails in one folder in the Lightbox and drag them onto the destination folder in the Folders List. To complete the move, click Yes in the Confirm Move dialog box that appears. The files are moved in Picasa as well as on your hard disk.

Confirm the move —————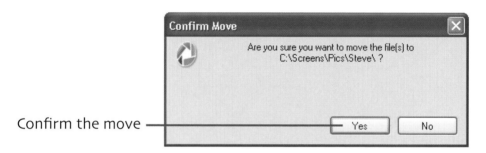

Move to New Folder is a more versatile version of the Split Folder Here command (described on page 52). Using this command, you can move any selected files from the current folder to a new folder.

1 From one folder, select the file(s) you want to move to a new folder. (To select multiple files, Ctrl-click or Shift-click their thumbnails.)

2 Choose File > Move to New Folder. The Folder Properties dialog box appears (see page 51).

3 Enter a name for the new folder and set a date. If you like, you can add information about where the photos were taken and a folder description. Click OK to transfer the selected images into the new folder.

Note that the new folder is created in parallel to the original folder; that is, both folders on disk will have the same parent folder.

organizing pictures

Rename a file. Using the Rename command, you can conveniently change the name of image files from within Picasa.

1 In the Lightbox, select the thumbnail of the file you want to rename, and then choose File > Rename (F2). The Rename Files dialog box appears.

2 Edit the name in the text box and click naming option check boxes, if desired.

The proposed filename is shown beneath the text box.

3 Click the Rename button to change the filename.

The new filename will appear in Picasa and in Windows.

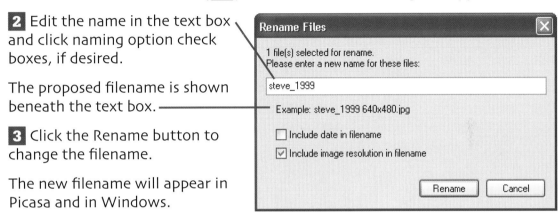

Rename Files ✕

1 file(s) selected for rename.
Please enter a new name for these files:

steve_1999

Example: steve_1999 640x480.jpg

☐ Include date in filename

☑ Include image resolution in filename

Rename   Cancel

Hide files. To eliminate the clutter in some folders, you can hide images. Hiding an image isn't as secure as placing it in a password-protected collection, but it does hide its thumbnail—until a command to reveal it is chosen.

To hide an image in the Lightbox, select its thumbnail and choose Picture > Hide, or right-click the image thumbnail and choose Hide from the pop-up menu.

To reveal all hidden thumbnails (regardless of the folders they're in), choose View > Hidden Pictures. A "ghost" thumbnail appears for each hidden image. To fully reveal a hidden image, right-click the ghost image and choose Unhide from the pop-up menu (or select the thumbnail and choose Picture > Unhide).

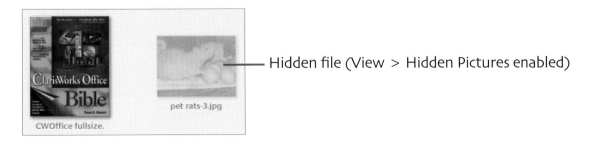

—— Hidden file (View > Hidden Pictures enabled)

organizing pictures

work with files (cont.)

Find a file on disk. **If you need to work directly with a particular file, you can instruct Picasa to quickly reveal its location on disk.**

1 Select an image thumbnail in the Lightbox.

2 Choose File > Locate on Disk, press [Ctrl] [Enter], or right-click the thumbnail and choose Locate on Disk from the pop-up menu that appears. The appropriate folder window opens with the file selected.

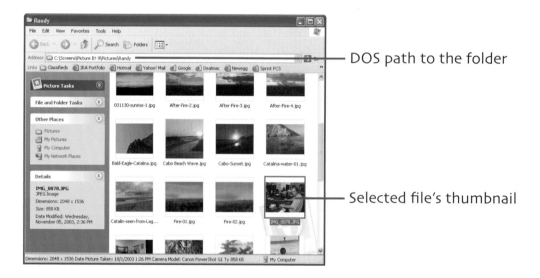

DOS path to the folder

Selected file's thumbnail

Delete a picture. **To delete a picture from disk, select its thumbnail in the Lightbox. Then choose File > Delete from Disk or press [Del].**

Confirm the deletion by clicking Yes in the Confirm Delete dialog box. The selected file is moved from its folder into the Recycle Bin. To complete the deletion, empty the Recycle Bin.

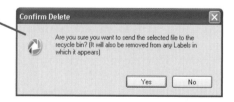

You can change your mind about deleting the file—before you empty the Recycle Bin, that is. Open the Recycle Bin, right-click the file's icon, and choose Restore from the pop-up menu that appears (see page 53).

organizing pictures

add identifiers

You can optionally add three kinds of identifiers to selected files to make them easier for you to find in searches: captions, star ratings, and keywords.

Add captions. Every image can have a caption—text that identifies the photo's subject, when/where it was taken, or something funny, for example.

1 Open the image for editing by double-clicking its thumbnail in the Lightbox.

2 If Make a caption! isn't visible beneath the image, click the Show/Hide Caption icon in the left-hand corner beneath the image.

Show/Hide caption   Make a caption!   Delete this caption

3 Click the Make a caption! text beneath the picture and type a caption, such as Evan and high school friends.

add identifiers (cont.)

Mark photos with a star. You can denote special photos by marking them with a star. What the star means is up to you. It could be used to mark your favorite pictures or only high-resolution ones, for example. A search option (discussed in Chapter 3) allows you to display only starred pictures.

To mark the selected photo(s) in the Picture Tray, click the Star icon. (Note that the Star icon is present both when working in the Library or when editing a picture.) To remove the star from selected images, click the Star icon again.

Star icon

Images in Picture Tray

Thumbnail after adding the star

Evan6_02b.jpg

Assign keywords. Another way to make it easier to find pictures with a Picasa search is to assign keywords to them. A keyword is a single word that describes an aspect of the picture, such as its subject. You can assign one or multiple keywords to an image.

1 Select an image thumbnail in the Light-box or open the image for editing.

2 Choose View > Keywords (Ctrl K). The Picasa: Keywords dialog box opens.

3 To assign a new keyword to the image, type it in the Add Keyword box and click the Add button. The keyword is added to the Keywords list for the picture.

4 To create additional keywords, repeat Step 3. When you're done, click OK.

Assign or remove an image's keywords in this dialog box.

organizing pictures

add folders and files

When you save new pictures to your hard disk, Picasa automatically adds them to its Library if the files are stored in a watched folder (see "Use the Folder Manager," earlier in this chapter). If you create a new folder on disk, you may have to visit the Folder Manager (Tools > Folder Manager) and select the new folder before Picasa notices and displays it—even if you place the new folder within another watched folder. If Picasa seems to be ignoring a new folder or files, you can add them to the Library as follows:

1 To add a folder (whether it's new or one that you previously removed from Picasa), choose File > Add Folder to Picasa. The Folder Manager appears.

2 Select the folder in the Folder Manager's Folder List, click the Watch for Changes radio button, and then click OK. The new folder will be scanned and added to the Picture Library's Folder List.

Folder List

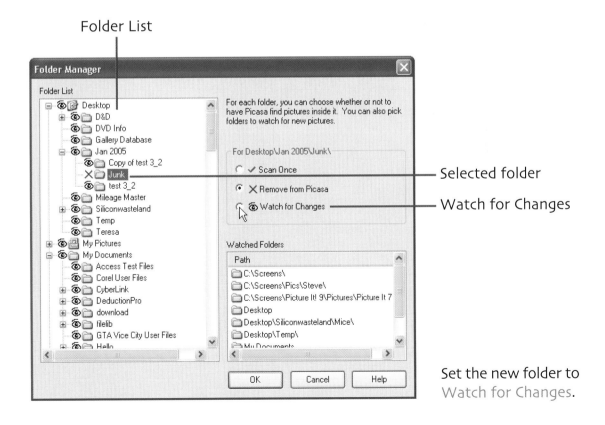

Selected folder

Watch for Changes

Set the new folder to Watch for Changes.

add folders and files (cont.)

1 To add a new file to Picasa, choose File > Add File to Picasa or press `Ctrl` `O`. An Open dialog box appears.

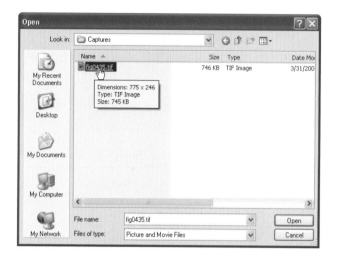

2 Using the Open dialog box's controls, navigate to the folder that contains the file you want to add to Picasa and click its filename. (If the dialog box doesn't immediately disappear, click the Open button.)

Folder ———

New file ———

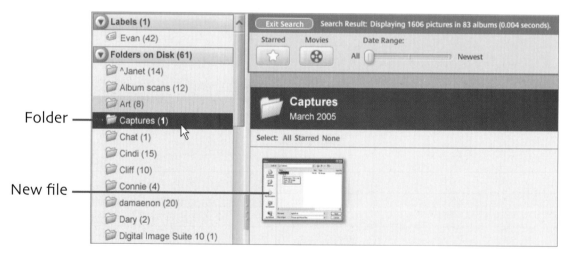

The file is recorded in Picasa. If its folder isn't already in the Folder List, the folder is added, too.

import pictures

Picasa can also import pictures from a variety of sources, such as a CD or DVD, digital camera or memory card reader, webcam, scanner, or a folder.

1 In many cases, Windows automatically recognizes when a new CD/DVD is inserted into a drive or a digital camera/memory card reader is connected. In those instances, a dialog box appears. Select Copy pictures to your computer and view them using Picasa 2, and then click OK.

If this dialog box doesn't appear or you want to copy images from a folder, webcam, or scanner, click Picasa's Import button, choose File > Import From, or press Ctrl M.

The importing screen (below) appears.

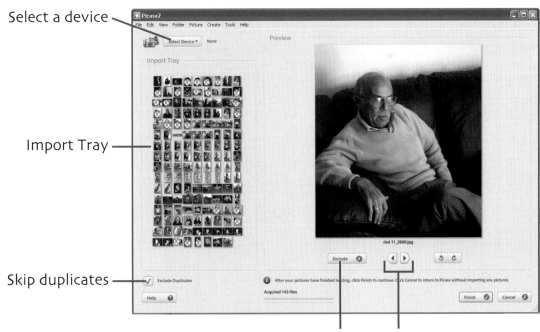

Select a device

Import Tray

Skip duplicates

Exclude/include this image   View Import Tray images

import pictures (cont.)

2 If you responded to a Windows dialog box in Step 1, Picasa automatically scans the device to display its image thumbnails. Otherwise, click the Select Device button and choose the appropriate device from the drop-down menu.

3 By default, Picasa excludes images that it knows are already on your hard disk, marking each one in the Input Tray with a red X. Review the images by clicking the right- and left-arrow buttons beneath the current image. To change the displayed image's exclusion status, click the Exclude button.

4 To import the images, click the Finish button. The Finish Importing dialog box appears.

5 Enter a name for the new folder that will receive the imported pictures, and click Finish.

The folder is created and added to the Folder List. All images — except those that you or Picasa excluded — appear in the folder.

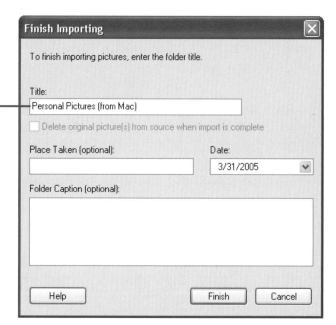

organizing pictures

extra bits

work with collections p. 46

- The Move to Collection menu can also be displayed by right-clicking anywhere in a folder's blue green band in the Light Box (to the right of the Folder List).

- Password-protection only protects collapsed collections in the Folder List. If you forget to collapse the collection, its folders and their contents will remain in full view of others—even if you quit and relaunch Picasa.

- Only collections that contain at least one folder are displayed in the Folder List. If you remove or move all folders from a collection, the collection name still appears in the Move to Collection submenu.

  To remove an empty collection, temporarily move a folder from the Other Stuff collection into the collection and then choose the Remove Collection command. The Other Stuff folder will automatically move back into the Other Stuff collection.

work with labels p. 49

- To change a label's description, select the label in the Folder List and choose Label > Edit Description. The Label Properties dialog box opens. You can also open this dialog box by double-clicking the label or by choosing Edit Label Description from the Actions button menu.

- You can add a single photo to a label by right-clicking the image and choosing the label name from the Add Label submenu. (This can be done with a thumbnail or when viewing/editing the image.)

- If you assign an image to a label with which it's already linked, Picasa ignores the assignment.

- You can also remove an image from a label by right-clicking its thumbnail or the image in Edit View. In the pop-up menu, choose Remove from Label.

- You can delete a label by right-clicking the label folder or its blue green title bar and choosing Delete Label in the pop-up menu that appears. You can also choose this command from the label's Actions button drop-down menu.

- To sort the pictures within the currently selected label, choose an order from the Label > Sort By submenu: Name, Date, or Size.

extra bits

work with folders p. 51

- If you use Windows to rename a folder, it will be updated in Picasa as soon as the change is noticed. (It isn't always immediate.)

- The Split Folder Here and Move to New Folder commands create new folders. If you later empty one of these folders in Picasa by moving or deleting the files, the folder will still exist on disk. Use Windows or Windows Explorer to delete the empty folder.

- When you create a new folder or change the name of an existing folder using Picasa, you will not be prevented from reusing a current folder's name. On disk, the new folder is distinguished from the original by adding a number to the end of its name, such as Mice_2. In Picasa, however, it will show two folders that are both named Mice.

- Many folders in the Other Stuff collection will be candidates for removal from Picasa. They often contain only sample images from programs, Web graphics, and pieces of Windows, for example.

- If you remove all folders from the Hidden Folders collection, the collection name will be removed from the Folders List. If you hide another folder, however, the collection will reappear. To alter the collection's password or to remove it, follow the instructions in "Password-protect a collection" (in this chapter).

- When Picasa initially scans your hard disk(s), it marks every image folder as Watch for Changes. To avoid unnecessary scanning, open the Folder Manager, select each folder that Picasa doesn't need to track, and select Remove from Picasa.

- To prevent a network drive from being continuously scanned, change its Folder Manager setting to Scan Once.

- When changing a folder's setting in Folder Manager, all its subfolders will receive the same setting. Thus, to avoid scanning Windows files, for example, just set the C:\WINDOWS directory to Remove from Picasa.

- To force Picasa to rescan a folder, change its Folder Manager setting to Remove from Picasa and click OK. Reopen the Folder Manager, restore the folder's original setting (Watch for Changes or Scan Once), and click OK.

organizing pictures

extra bits

work with files p. 56

- You can use the Rename command to rename multiple selected files, too. See "Batch Edit" in Chapter 5 for the file-naming conventions that are used.

- If a folder no longer contains any Picasa-viewable image files, it is removed from the Folder List. If you want to work with that folder (to delete it or examine its other contents, for example), you'll have to do so using Windows or another program. To make the folder accessible to Picasa again, add an image file to the folder.

add identifiers p. 59

- You can edit an existing caption, but only from the end of the text string. Press (Backspace) as many times as necessary to delete the incorrect letters at the end and then type the replacement text.

- To completely erase a caption (either to eliminate it or to start over), click the Delete this caption icon beneath the picture.

- Keywords and captions are saved as part of an image's data. Some of this text data can be viewed in the file's Properties dialog box (choose Picture > Properties) and in some other programs, too.

- Picasa 2 does not present a list of your keywords when you try to add one to a new image. However, as you type, Picasa will automatically suggest existing keywords that begin with the letters you're typing.

add folders and files p. 61

- Photos that you receive in Hello (see Chapter 10) are automatically added to the From Hello collection. Each friend gets his or her own primary folder in this collection, named with the person's Hello user name.

5. editing photos: basic fixes and tuning

Few photos start out as perfect. You can modify pictures using the tools on the panel that appears when you open a picture in Edit View. To edit an image, double-click its Picture Library thumbnail, or select its thumbnail and choose View > Edit View ([Ctrl][3]). When you're done editing, click the Back To Library button.

In this chapter, we'll examine edits that you can perform using the Basic Fixes and Tuning tabs of the panel. In Chapter 6, you'll learn to apply the photographic-style filters on the Effects tab to your pictures.

No matter which tab you're on, the bottom of the panel has two buttons: Undo and Redo. Click them to reverse the effect of the most recent edit (Undo) or reapply the most recent effect you've removed with Undo (Redo). The button labels change to reflect the specific edit/command you can Undo or Redo. Because Picasa tracks all edits for each image, you can click Undo repeatedly to remove a series of edits—all the way back to the original image, if you like.

The edit sequence is stored with the picture. If you open it at a later date in Picasa, you can still use the Undo button to step back through your edits.

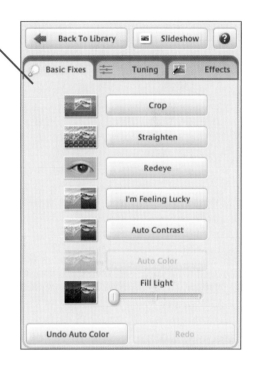

Basic Fixes tab (Edit View)

Undo and Redo buttons

one-button fixes

Three adjustments on the Basic Fixes tab are applied with a single button click: I'm Feeling Lucky, Auto Contrast, and Auto Color. The Rotate buttons (found to the right of the Picture Tray) are also one-click tools.

I'm Feeling Lucky. For many pictures that aren't quite up to snuff, I'm Feeling Lucky is the first adjustment you should try. It attempts to set image contrast and colors to optimal levels. When applied, you'll often note that soft, slightly fuzzy digital photos become clearer and sharper. (If you're familiar with Photoshop, this command is similar to its Auto Levels.)

Original photo

"I'm Feeling Lucky" applied

Auto Contrast. Click this button to set brightness and contrast to optimal levels—without altering the image colors. Adjusting the contrast can bring out detail in dark areas, as well as add definition to slightly washed out areas.

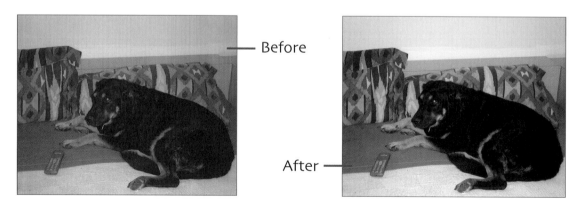
— Before

After —

Auto Color. Click this button to adjust the colors of an image to what Picasa considers optimal. This tool can be very useful for removing a color cast that resulted from shooting indoors under poor lighting conditions, for example.

This unedited shot has a warm, pinkish/flesh-colored cast.

After applying the Auto Color correction, the color cast has been neutralized—resulting in a cooler image with more natural skin tones.

Rotate counter-clockwise

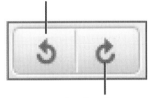

Rotate clockwise

Rotate. This pair of buttons (found below the picture) enables you to flip the current picture's orientation from portrait to landscape and vice versa. Like other edits, the new orientation is saved with the picture.

Original

Rotated

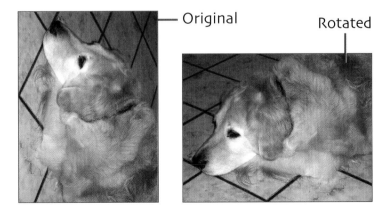

A photo shot by holding the camera sideways can easily be fixed by clicking a Rotate button.

editing photos: basic fixes and tuning

Crop

Camera shots aren't always perfectly framed. When you examine them, you might find that they're off-center or contain extraneous objects on one or more edges, for example. You can correct these photos with the Crop tool, selecting a rectangular portion that you want to keep while trimming away all material outside the selected area. You can crop any image to match a common photo paper size or create a custom-sized image.

1 Open a picture for editing, click the Basic Fixes tab, and click the Crop button.

2 Click a radio button on the Crop Picture panel to set the image's dimensions.

3 Click and drag in the picture to set the crop area. (If you selected any option other than Manual in Step 2, the dragged area will maintain constant proportions that correspond to the selected dimensions.)

Crop Picture panel

Click to show selected area as a new picture

Area to be cropped

4 Optional: To change the size of the selection rectangle, drag one of its edges or corners. To change the position of the selection rectangle, click anywhere in its center and drag it to a new location. To switch from a portrait to a landscape selection rectangle, click the Rotate button. To see what the selected area will look like when cropped, click the Preview button.

5 When you're satisfied with the selection, click Apply.

The cropped image replaces the original in Edit View and in the Picture Library.

If you decide that you'd like to restore the original, open it for editing again and click the Undo Crop button at the bottom of the Edit panel.

Straighten

Have you ever squeezed off a quick shot only to discover that the horizon or another major element wasn't horizontal? Using the Straighten tool, you can easily correct this occasional problem.

1 Open a picture for editing, click the Basic Fixes tab, and click the Straighten button. A grid is superimposed over the picture, and controls appear at the bottom.

Straighten controls ———

2 Drag the slider at the bottom of the picture to rotate the image. You can use the grid lines to help you horizontally align on any component. When you're satisfied, click Apply.

Note: Straightening a picture crops it at the same time. If key elements are at the edges of the crooked photo, you may lose them.

Redeye

When you take pictures using a flash, your subjects can sometimes be afflicted with red eye, an annoying condition in which the iris (the colored part of the eye) glows an eerie red. You can use the Redeye tool to change the eyes to a more natural color, salvaging an otherwise unusable shot.

1 Open the picture for editing, click the Basic Fixes tab, and click the Redeye button. The Redeye Repair panel appears.

2 Drag a selection rectangle around one of the eyes and then release the mouse button. Picasa removes the red from the selected area. Repeat this procedure for the other eye. If red remains in either or both eyes, you can repeat the process.

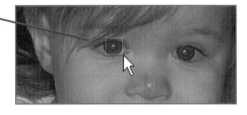

3 When you're satisfied with the results, click Apply.

Note: When viewing the edited photo, increase the magnification so you can closely examine the eyes. If they still contain red, repeat the Redeye Repair.

Fill Light

Photos shot indoors—especially those taken at night without the benefit of a flash—often contain areas that are too dark. By applying the Fill Light tool, you may be able to improve these photos by brightening the dark areas without washing out the lighter areas.

1 Open the picture for editing and click the Basic Fixes tab.

 **2** Slowly drag the Fill Light slider to the right, observing its effect as you drag.

Original image

After applying Fill Light

3 When satisfied, click the Back To Library button above the Basic Fixes panel.

editing photos: basic fixes and tuning

Tuning controls

The Tuning controls work differently than controls on the Basic Fixes and Effects tabs. All tuning adjustments are treated as a single edit and are reversed by clicking one button: Undo Tuning. Use the Tuning tab to apply multiple edits or adjust an already edited image. When done, click another tab or the Back To Library button.

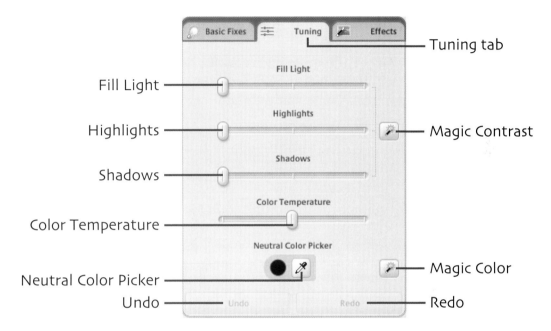

Magic Contrast. This is the same as the Auto Contrast button (Basic Fixes tab).

Magic Color. This is the same as the Auto Color button (Basic Fixes tab).

Fill Light. This is the same as the Fill Light control (Basic Fixes tab).

Highlights and Shadows. When used together, these controls enable you to manually adjust an image's contrast and brightness.

Color Temperature. Move this slider to adjust a picture's "warmth." Drag to the left to make it cooler or to the right to make it warmer.

Neutral Color Picker. Click the Eyedropper icon and then click a gray or white area in the image. Doing so sets that color as neutral for the image, allowing Picasa to automatically adjust all other colors.

Batch Edit

Picasa also supports batch commands (drawn from edit procedures on the Basic Fixes and Effects tabs) that you can apply to multiple images simultaneously.

Note: Although there is a batch Undo command, it removes all edits from the selected image(s). To selectively reverse the effects of one or more batch edits, open each affected image—one by one—and click the Undo button as many times as needed to step back through the edits.

1 Within a single folder, select the images to which you want to apply the batch edits, displaying them in the Picture Tray. (If the images are currently in multiple folders, copy them to a single folder first.)

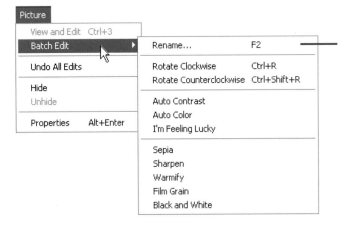

2 Choose a command from the Picture > Batch Edit submenu.

The chosen edit is applied to all selected images. Their thumbnails update to reflect the edit procedure.

3 Optional: If you wish, you can choose additional Batch Edit commands.

editing photos: basic fixes and tuning

The Rename command is especially handy for renaming a folder of imported digital photos, since each normally has a useless name, such as P5120001.jpg. When renaming files, the first file receives only the base name, such as flower. jpg. Subsequent files in the group receive a sequential number in the form flower-1.jpg, flower-2.jpg, and so on.

1 With the image thumbnails selected, choose Picture > Batch Edit > Rename or press F2. The Rename Files dialog box appears.

2 Type a base name in the text box. To include the date and/or image resolution as part of the filename, click the appropriate check box or boxes.

The selected naming conventions are reflected in the Example filename.

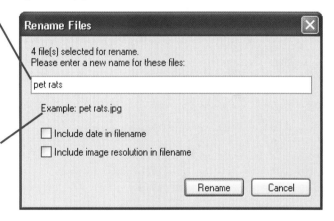

3 Click the Rename button to complete the process.

Remove batch edits. To remove the batch edits you just applied, select one or more of the edited images in the Picture Library and then choose Picture > Undo All Edits. Click Yes in the Confirm dialog box that appears.

Confirm the
Undo All Edits

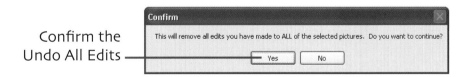

editing photos: basic fixes and tuning

extra bits

one-button fixes p. 70

- Like all edits, the effects of these fixes are cumulative. If you change your mind after applying an effect, click the Undo button before applying a different effect.

- Digital photos can often benefit from the application of I'm Feeling Lucky, Auto Contrast, or Auto Color. You may want to try these tools first and then apply manual tuning as needed.

- There is no Undo for a rotation. Click the opposite Rotate button to reverse the rotation.

- You can also rotate images without leaving the Picture Library. Select their thumbnails and click one of the Rotate buttons at the bottom of the screen.

Crop p. 72

- A Manual crop is best reserved only for pictures destined for on-screen viewing. Unless you crop to a standard paper size, manual cropping often results in extra white space around the edges of the print.

Redeye p. 75

- If you Undo a Redeye correction, the fix cannot later be reapplied by clicking Redo. You'll have to make the Redeye correction again.

- Be careful not to select too much area around the red. Doing so can result in a strange, unwanted effect that's similar to colored eye liner.

Tuning controls p. 77

- Think of the Tuning controls as Picasa's advanced editing tools. Until you become familiar with the ways they interact with one another, you may prefer to stick to the simpler corrections on the Basic Fixes tab.

Batch Edit p. 78

- Not all batch edits can be undone with Undo All Edits. Reverse a Rotate command by choosing the opposite command. To restore the filename to a renamed image, select the image in the Picture Library and choose File > Rename.

6. editing photos: effects

An effect simulates a photographic filter. To apply an effect to the current image, click the effect's icon on the Effects tab. Effects are applied to entire images.

Each effect icon shows an approximation of the effect it will produce when applied to the current image. The top five icons each have a tiny 1 in the lower-right corner, denoting that their effect is applied instantly; all other effects require you to select options or adjust settings. To remove the most recently applied effect, click the Undo button. To reapply a removed effect, click Redo.

Effects tab

Effect icons

Remove effect (Undo)

Reapply effect (Redo)

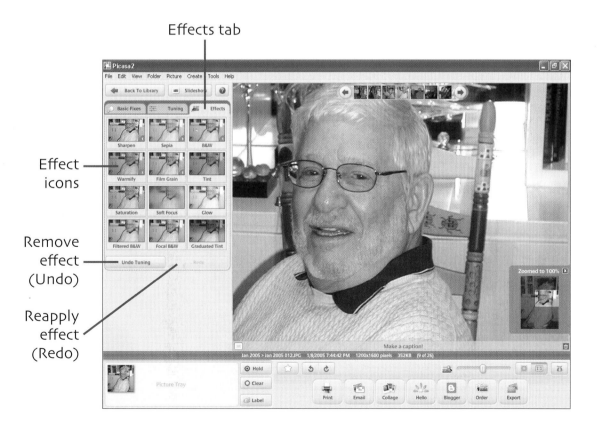

apply one-click effects

The first five effects can be applied by simply clicking an icon. To see the impact of each effect, you can compare its picture to the original on the previous page.

Sharpen. This effect increases the amount of fine detail visible in an image. Because digital photos and scans are often slightly fuzzy, you'll want to apply this effect to many shots. While Sharpen can be applied multiple times to the same image, more than once is typically overkill. That is, you probably won't be able to use Sharpen to salvage an extremely blurry shot.

Sharpen

Sepia. Apply the Sepia effect to transform an image into an antique-style duotone photo. The result is a black-and-white image with a brownish tint.

B&W. Use the B&W effect to turn any color image into a black-and-white photograph.

Sepia

B&W

editing photos: effects

Warmify. This effect adds 'warmth' to a photo. It's very useful when people appear pale (often due to poor lighting).

Film Grain. Use this artistic effect to simulate the mottled, graininess of a photo shot on film. The effect is especially noticeable in solid-colored areas, such as the gray wall.

editing photos: effects

Tint

Apply Tint to create a duotone using a color of your choice. You can optionally preserve some of the original colors of the image, while applying the overall tint.

1 Open the picture for editing, click the Effects tab, and click the Tint icon.

Effects tab

Tint icon

Original image

Color Preservation slider

Pick Color box

Current tint color

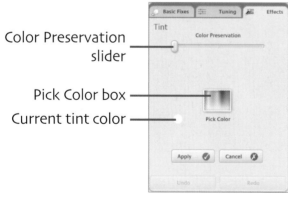

2 To accept the default tint color (white), adjust the Color Preservation slider to indicate the amount of original colors to retain, and then click Apply.

Otherwise, to select a different tint color, adjust the Color Preservation slider (if desired). Then click in the Pick Color box to set the initial tint shade.

3 To preview the effect of different colors, drag the eye-dropper over the color picker or the color hexagons. As you drag, the picture's tint automatically changes to reflect the new color. Click a color hexagon or a spot on the color picker to set the color.

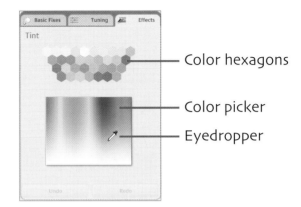

Color hexagons

Color picker

Eyedropper

The Step 2 screen reappears.

4 Make a final adjustment to the Color Preservation slider, if necessary.

No color preservation

50% preservation

Full preservation

5 Click Apply to apply the chosen Tint settings to the image, or click Cancel if you've changed your mind.

editing photos: effects

Saturation

Use the Saturation effect to increase or decrease the richness or density of an image's colors.

1 Open the picture for editing, click the Effects tab, and click the Saturation icon. The Saturation panel appears.

Saturation panel

2 Drag the Amount slider to set the degree of color saturation. Drag to the left to reduce saturation or to the right to increase it.

3 When you're satisfied with the effect, click Apply. Or click Cancel if you've changed your mind.

Amount slider

By increasing saturation, you may be able to change an overcast scene into a cheery, more colorful one, for example.

editing photos: effects

Soft Focus

Use Soft Focus to leave a portion of a photo in sharp focus, while surrounding it with out-of-focus material. (This effect is often used to frame the happy couple in wedding photos, for example.)

1 Open the picture for editing, click the Effects tab, and click the Soft Focus icon. The Soft Focus panel appears.

Soft Focus panel

2 Center the crosshair cursor over the area you want to keep in focus.

editing photos: effects

3 Adjust the Size and Amount sliders as desired.

The Size slider determines the size of the in-focus area surrounding the cross-hair cursor. The Amount slider determines the "fuzziness" (or softness) of the soft focus effect.

Size slider   Amount slider

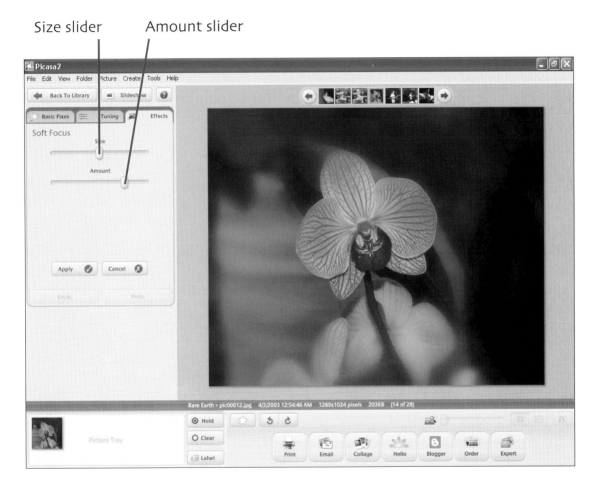

4 When you're satisfied with the effect, click Apply. Or click Cancel if you've changed your mind.

Glow

Glow is an unusual, special-purpose effect. It's similar to Soft Focus, but affects only a photo's white areas.

1 Open the picture for editing, click the Effects tab, and click the Glow icon. The Glow panel appears. ————————

2 To set the amount and size of the glow effect, adjust the Intensity and Radius sliders.

3 When you're satisfied with the effect, click Apply. Or click Cancel if you've changed your mind.

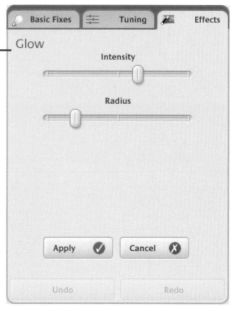

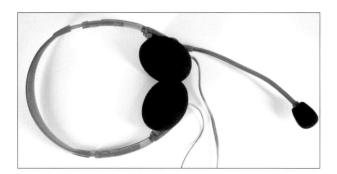

Original photo

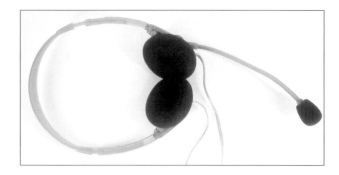

Glow applied

Filtered B&W

Filtered B&W is a controlled color to black-and-white conversion. Rather than perform an exact conversion (as is done when applying the B&W effect; see page 82), Filtered B&W is accomplished by simulating the use of a color filter with black-and-white film. The resulting image depends on the colors in the original photo and the color filter selected.

1 Open the picture for editing, click the Effects tab, and click Filtered B&W. In the Filtered B&W panel, click in the Pick Color box to set the shade of the initial color filter.

2 Move the eyedropper over the color picker or the color hexagons. As you move, the photo changes to reflect the color's effect. Click a color hexagon or a spot on the color picker to select the color.

3 When you're satisfied with the effect, click Apply. Or click Cancel if you've changed your mind.

Original color image

Filtered B&W

Focal B&W

Use Focal B&W to create a black-and-white image from a color photo while leaving a selected, circular area in color. Applied carefully, this unusual effect can create the appearance of a partially hand-colored photo.

1 Open the picture for editing, click the Effects tab, and then click the Focal B&W icon.

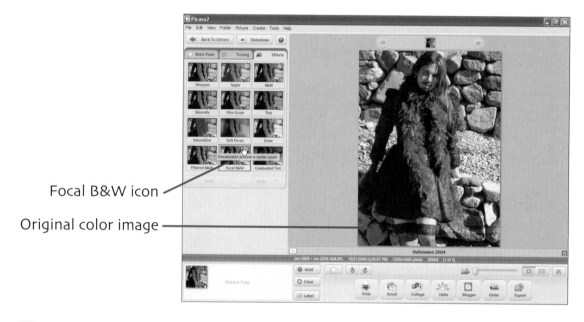

Focal B&W icon

Original color image

2 The Focal B&W panel appears and the image is converted to black-and-white (see next page). Move the focal point (the yellow crosshair cursor), centering it over the area that will retain its color.

3 Adjust the Size and Sharpness controls as desired.

The Size control setting determines the focal point's radius. Use the Sharpness control to feather the focal point circle's edges (when moved to the left) or to display hard edges (when moved to the right).

4 When you're satisfied with the effect, click Apply. Or click Cancel if you've changed your mind.

editing photos: effects

Focal B&W panel   Focal point cursor

Apply the current
settings to the image

This photo was selected because it's almost perfect for the Focal B&W effect.
The dress and most of the background elements are black, white, or a shade of
gray. When applying Focal B&W effect to a typical color photo, you'll find it
difficult to colorize only a single item (as was done with the feather boa).

Graduated Tint

Use Graduated Tint to apply a color gradient tint, starting from the top of the image. Because the tint is always applied from the top down, it's very useful for dramatically altering the color of the sky. Graduated Tint can be applied with a horizontal or angled bottom edge.

1 Open the picture for editing, click the Effects tab, and click the Graduated Tint icon.

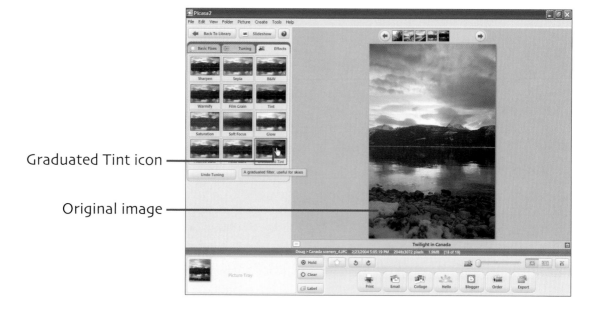

Graduated Tint icon ——

Original image ——

2 In the Graduated Tint panel, click in the Pick Color box to set the initial tint shade.

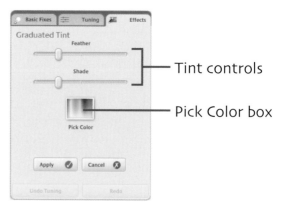

—— Tint controls

—— Pick Color box

editing photos: effects

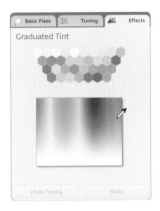

3 To preview the effect of different colors, move the eyedropper over the color picker or the color hexagons. As you move the eyedropper, the picture's tint automatically changes to reflect the new color. Click a color hexagon or a spot on the color picker to set the color.

4 Position the crosshair to set the bottom edge of the effect. Place it in the center to create a horizontal edge; place it to the left or right to create an angled edge.

5 Adjust the Feather and Shade sliders, as desired. (Shade sets the darkness or intensity of the tint color; Feather sets the edge definition.) When you're satisfied with the effect, click Apply. Or click Cancel if you've changed your mind.

Tint controls ——

Crosshair cursor ——

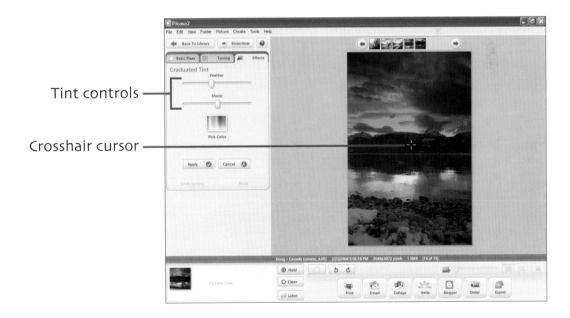

editing photos: effects

extra bits

apply one-click effects p. 82

- Like other edits, applying multiple effects is cumulative. Unless that's what you're trying to achieve, click the Undo button at the bottom of the Effects tab to remove the most recently applied effect before applying a new one.

- You can apply one photo's edits to another photo. Select the edited photo and choose Edit > Copy All Effects. Select the target photo and choose Edit > Paste All Effects.

- Many digital cameras provide settings that let you shoot sepia-toned or black-and-white photos.

Tint p. 84

- Use Tint sparingly. There are few non-artistic instances in which photos look good with an overall bluish or reddish cast.

- To create a duotone photo with Tint, move the Color Preservation slider all the way to the left.

- When applying effects such as Tint, the process isn't necessarily as straightforward as "Do A, do B, and click Apply." You're free to select a color and adjust controls in whatever order works for you, as well as to repeatedly switch back and forth between these processes as needed.

Saturation p. 86

- If too much Saturation is applied, areas of the photo will look blotchy. Move the Amount slider slightly to the left if this occurs.

Soft Focus p. 88

- If you apply Soft Focus to the elements closest to the camera, you can simulate depth of field. This is an excellent way to attain more natural-looking photos from fixed-focus cameras that are focused for infinity.

7. printing and emailing photos

In this chapter, you'll learn about two important Picasa capabilities: printing pictures stored in the Library—whether they're originals or ones you've edited with Picasa—and emailing pictures to relatives, friends, and classmates.

You'll find Picasa is one of the easiest programs for generating nice prints in sizes and layouts ranging from wallet to 8" x 10" (full page). It even warns if you try to print an image whose resolution isn't sufficient for the chosen print size.

It's simple to email pictures directly from Picasa, too. Options allow you to email one or multiple images in their original size or reduced to a preset maximum, as well as to send them in storybook format (embedded in the message in a vertical array).

Messages in storybook format contain a series of labeled images like this one. You can edit the default message Subject, text, and image labels, if you like.

Note: Be sure to read "E-Mail Options" in Chapter 2. The E-Mail Options determine everything important about the format, size, and quality of pictures you send.

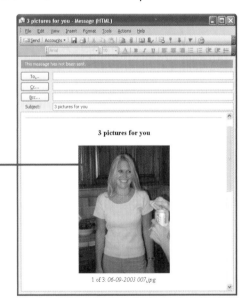

print photos

Use the Print command to print your favorite photos to any printer that's connected to your PC or available on your network.

1 Select the picture(s) you want to print. (To print pictures from multiple folders, select photos from the first folder, click the Hold button, select photos from another folder, click Hold, and so on.) Thumbnails of the selected pictures appear in the Picture Tray.

Note: Although you can print multiple pictures simultaneously, all selected images will use the same print settings.

2 Click the Print button, choose File > Print, or press Ctrl P. The Preview/Print Layout screen appears.

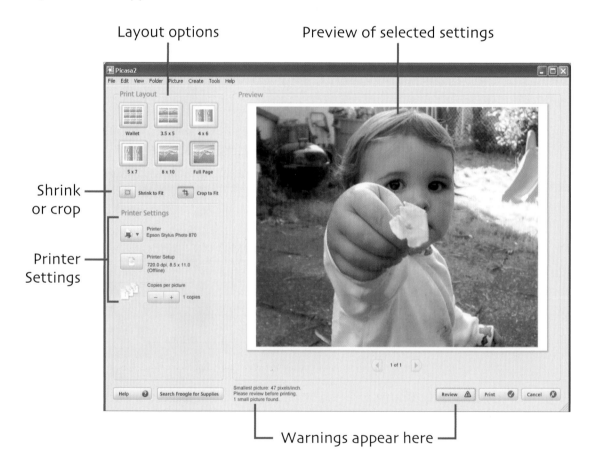

Layout options   Preview of selected settings

Shrink or crop

Printer Settings

Warnings appear here

3 Ensure that the correct printer is shown in the Printer Settings area.

To switch printers, click the Printer button and select a printer name from the list of installed printers. (Note that non-printing devices, such as screen capture programs and fax modems, may also be listed.)

4 Check the resolution (dpi) and paper size listed beside the Printer Setup button. To change or review printer options (such as paper size and type, print quality, and color versus black-and-white), click the Printer Setup button. Make any necessary changes in the Document Properties dialog box and click OK.

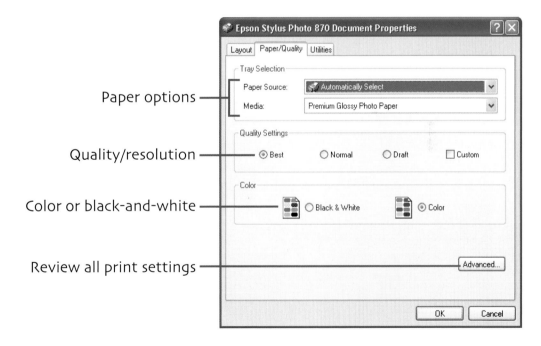

Paper options

Quality/resolution

Color or black-and-white

Review all print settings

Note: Click the Advanced button to set a specific print quality, such as 1440 dpi.

print photos (cont.)

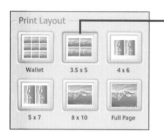

5 Click a layout icon at the top of the Print Layout area to specify the size of each print. Picasa updates the Preview area to show how the selected photo(s) will be placed on the paper.

6 The Shrink to Fit and Crop to Fit buttons determine how the selected images are fitted on the page. (Shrink to Fit shrinks each image as necessary, but retains its original proportions. Crop to Fit places each image at exactly the selected size, throwing away detail at the edges, if needed.) Click one of the two buttons; the Preview area updates to reflect your choice.

7 To specify the number of copies of each picture to print, click the ⊕ or ⊖ button. ―――――――――

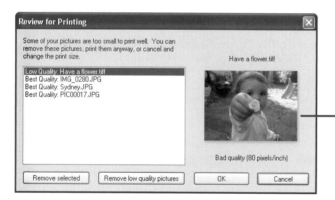

8 If the quality of any picture is marginal when printed at the selected size, a warning appears at the bottom of the screen. Click the Review button. The Review for Printing dialog box lists the pictures to be printed and the quality of each when printed at the current size.

You can remove any problem pictures by selecting each one and clicking Remove selected. To simultaneously remove all low-quality images, click Remove low quality pictures. Click OK to close the dialog box. When only Best Quality images remain, the caution icon is removed from the Review button.

9 Ensure that the printer is on and ready to print. Click Print to start printing.

print a contact sheet

When working with film, a contact sheet is a special printout that shows every picture on the roll as a set of negative-sized images. A contact sheet serves as a handy reference to a roll's contents. In Picasa, you can print a contact sheet of any individual folder or label.

1 In the Picture Library, select a folder or label from the Folder List.

2 Choose Folder > Print Contact Sheet ([Ctrl][Shift][P]). The Preview/Print Layout screen appears.

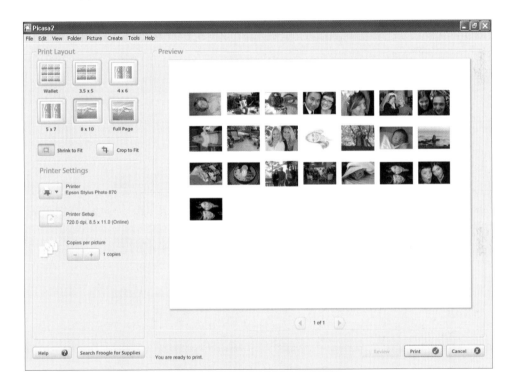

3 Make any desired changes to the options in the Printer Settings area. But do not select a Print Layout size; doing so will take you out of Contact Sheet mode.

4 You should normally select Shrink to Fit to ensure that you'll see each picture in its entirety. However, you can select Crop to Fit, if you prefer.

5 Ensure that the printer is on and ready to print. Then click Print.

order professional prints

Whether it's because you don't have a color printer or you're accustomed to the prints you get with processed film, you can still obtain professional prints from your favorite digital photos. Picasa 2 provides Web links to five digital image processing firms: Wal-Mart, Ofoto (Kodak), Ritz Camera/Wolf Camera, Shutterfly, and Snapfish. After creating an account with one of these companies, you can upload images from Picasa and order prints, posters, or photo gift items (such as calendars, mugs, and mouse pads).

1 Select the pictures you want to print, adding them to the Picture Tray.

2 Click the Order button (bottom of the screen), choose File > Order Prints, or press ⌨Ctrl⌨T. The Picasa Prints & Products screen appears.

Processing firms

3 Click the Choose button for the provider you'd like to use. The Order Prints window for the chosen provider appears.

4 If you already have an account with the provider, enter your login information and click OK.

If you don't have an account, click the Create an account text link. A sign-up Web page appears in your default browser. Enter the requested information to create your new account. When you're finished, close the browser and repeat Steps 3 and 4.

5 After successfully logging in to your account, a browser window will open to the provider's site. All images in the Picture Tray will automatically be uploaded. Follow the provider's instructions to organize and view your stored photos, allow friends to view them, or order prints.

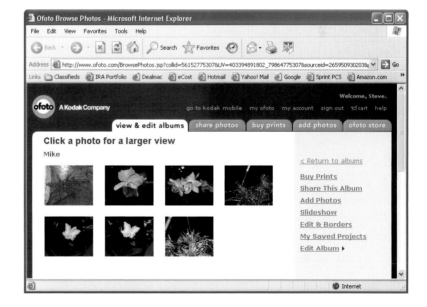

Images uploaded to Ofoto are organized in albums. Click tabs, links, and thumbnails to perform various activities.

printing and emailing photos   **103**

email photos

From within Picasa, you can generate email messages that include picture attachments from your Picasa library. It doesn't matter whether the attached photos have been edited with Picasa or are unaltered originals.

The way Picasa handles attached photos is determined by settings on the E-Mail tab of the Options window (see "E-Mail Options" in Chapter 2 for instructions).

1 Select the picture(s) you want to send, adding them to the Picture Tray.

2 Click the Email button (at the bottom of the screen), choose File > E-Mail, or press Ctrl E.

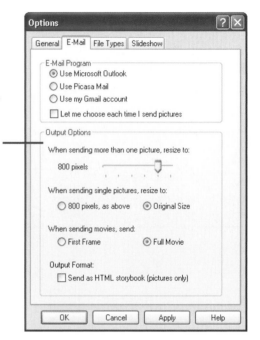

3 If Let me choose each time I send pictures is checked in the Options dialog box (shown above), the Select Email dialog box appears.

Click the email program you'll use to send these pictures. (Your default email program should be the first one listed.)

4 A message is generated in the selected email program. All images in the Picture Tray are attached to or embedded in the message, depending on the settings in the Options dialog box. Specify the message recipient(s), edit the default text as necessary, and send the message.

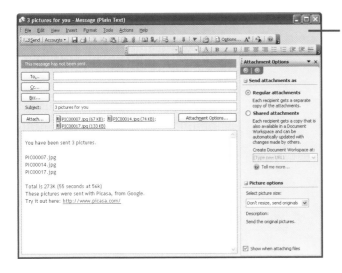

This Microsoft Outlook message contains three attached photos, resized as directed in the Options dialog box.

If you have a Hello account (see Chapter 10), you can use Picasa Mail to send photos. On the Picasa Mail login screen, enter your Hello user name and password.

In the message that's generated, enter the recipient's email address, edit the Subject and message text as you wish, and click the Send button.

printing and emailing photos

extra bits

print photos p. 98

- Because all selected photos will use the same print settings, you'll sometimes find it easier to print fewer pictures at a time. Doing so will allow you to print them in different sizes, properly handle varying image quality, and print in landscape or portrait mode, as needed.

- One way to improve a picture's print quality is to print it at a smaller size. For example, while a 2 megapixel photo might result in a marginally acceptable 8" x 10" print, a 5" x 7" or 4" x 6" print will be better.

- Photo paper is expensive. If part of a page is blank, you can fill it by adding more photos or by increasing the number of copies of each photo.

- If your printer doesn't print, ensure that it's on, online (ready to print), and has paper. Note that many inkjets will refuse to print if any of its ink cartridges are empty.

- If you're tired of paying through the nose for ink cartridges, you may want to explore the world of compatible cartridges. Go to http://dealink.com for sources of inexpensive ink cartridges.

order professional prints p. 102

- Registration at provider sites is free. Thus, there's no harm in registering at several sites. That way, you can explore each one's options, prices, and free features before ordering.

- Although it's convenient to log in from Picasa, you can also go directly to a provider's site by entering its address in your Web browser. If you don't need to upload photos in the current session, there's no need to enter the site through Picasa.

- Before logging onto a provider site, be sure that the Picture Tray doesn't contain extraneous photos. All photos in the Picture Tray will automatically be uploaded to the site when you log in.

email photos p. 104

- To send Picasa-edited photos directly from within your email program, use Save a Copy (Chapter 9) to create a new JPEG that contains the edits. Then attach the copy to your email message.

- If you're sending storybooks, be sure to set your email program's default message format to HTML.

8. special features and projects

In this chapter, you'll learn how to use several Picasa features to create fun and useful projects. After selecting pictures and setting a few simple options, you can generate a Desktop background, screen saver, movie, photo Web page, multi-page poster, or image collage.

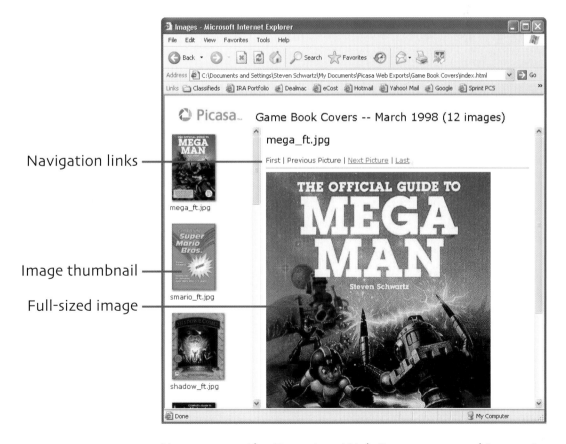

Navigation links

Image thumbnail

Full-sized image

You can use the Export as Web Page command to create a Web page with clickable thumbnails.

save image as Desktop

Are you tired of the pictures and patterns Microsoft provides for the Desktop background (also called wallpaper)? Using Picasa, you can transform any image in the library into your new Desktop background.

1 Select a photo thumbnail in the Picture Library or open the image for editing.

New Desktop image

2 Choose Create > Set as Desktop. Click Yes in the Confirm dialog box that appears. The image becomes the new Desktop background/wallpaper.

In the Display control panel, the file is named picasabackground. Each time you create a new Desktop in Picasa, the existing picasabackground file is replaced.

Desktop preview

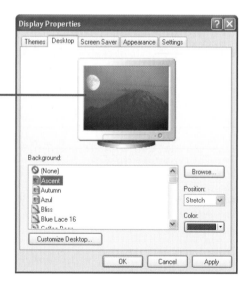

If you later want to restore your previous Desktop or select one from the background images supplied with Windows, open the Display control panel. Click the Desktop tab, select an image or pattern from the Background list, and click Apply. If the image is satisfactory, click OK.

create a screen saver

You can also use Picasa to create a slideshow-style screen saver from any group of photos.

1 Select the photos you want to include in the screen saver.

2 Choose Create > Screensaver. Copies of the selected pictures are saved in a new Picture Library folder named Screensaver.

The Display Properties control panel appears, open to the Screen Saver tab. The new screen saver (Picasa2 Screen Saver) is automatically selected.

Selected screen saver
Settings button

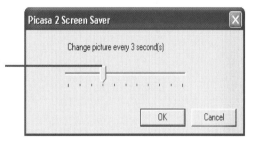

3 Click the Settings button. Drag the slider in the Picasa 2 Screen Saver dialog box to set the delay time between pictures. Then click OK to return to the Display Properties control panel.

4 Click OK to dismiss the Display Properties control panel, accepting the new screen saver.

make a movie

Another cool feature is Picasa's ability to turn any set of photos into a movie that can be played with Windows Media Player or a similar utility. Rather than generate a simple slideshow movie, each image is panned to simulate motion.

1 Select the images to be used, adding them to the Picture Tray in the order in which they'll appear in the movie.

2 Choose Create > Movie. In the Create Movie dialog box, set the Delay between pictures (1–5 seconds) and select the Movie size (in pixels). Click OK.

3 The Video Compression dialog box opens. Select a compression codec from the Compressor drop-down list. Click OK to create the movie.

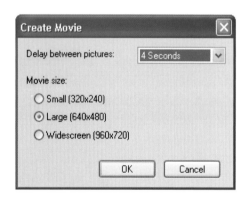

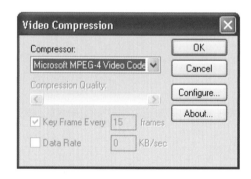

4 When Picasa finishes rendering the movie, it is saved using the name of the folder from which the last image was drawn, such as Desktop.avi. The folder in which the movie is stored opens automatically. Cick the movie's file icon to view the movie.

Note: When selecting a compression codec, steer clear of Full Frames (Uncompressed). It can generate huge movies—often 100 MB or larger! You may want to start by experimenting with the various Microsoft MPEG-4 codecs.

make a Web page

If you have photos you'd like to share with others on the Web (assuming you have access to Web space), you can use the Export as Web Page command to effortlessly create the page. The resulting HTML and image files can be uploaded to a Web server.

1 Select the images to be included on the Web page, displaying them in order in the Picture Tray. (All selected images must be from the same folder.)

2 Choose Folder > Export as Web Page or press Ctrl W.

3 In the Export as Web Page dialog box, select a picture size, enter a title for the Web page, and specify a folder in which to save the HTML and image files. (To select a folder other than the proposed one, click Browse.) Click Next.

Select a folder ———

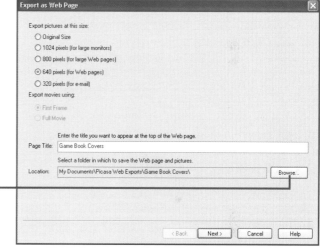

Templates   Preview

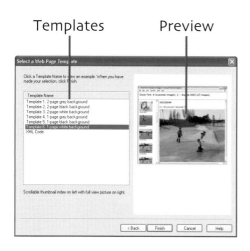

4 Select a layout from the template list. Click Finish to create the Web page.

Picasa opens the generated Web page in your default browser (see page 107).

create a poster

If you have a photo you'd like to print on paper that's larger than your printer can handle, you can use the Make a Poster command to split it into multiple images you can print and tape together. A poster-sized photo is a great item for special events, such as birthday parties, wedding receptions, and anniversaries.

1 Select a photo thumbnail in the Picture Library or open the image for editing.

2 Choose Create > Make a Poster.

3 In the Poster Settings dialog box, select a Poster size (enlargement percentage) and a Paper size. If you want the pages to include overlapping areas to make it simpler to match them up, click the Overlap tiles check box.

Poster Settings — dialog box

4 Click OK to create the new images. Picasa stores them in the same folder as the original. Print the poster pieces. Tape them together or mount them on a flat surface, such as a piece of tagboard.

No overlap

Overlapping — tiles

special features and projects

make a collage

Collage is one of Picasa's most interesting features. You can use it to combine multiple images into a picture pile (Polaroid-style photos) or a multiple exposure (one picture superimposed over another), for example.

1 Select the pictures from which you want to create a collage, adding them to the Picture Tray.

2 Choose Create > Picture Collage or click the Collage button. The Make Collage dialog box appears. As you make new choices, the preview area updates to show their effect.

Picture Pile example

3 Choose a collage style from the Type pop-up menu: Picture Pile, Picture Grid, Contact Sheet, or Multi-Exposure.

4 Choose a background color or image from the Options pop-up menu.

5 Optional: To specify where to store the resulting collage (different from the proposed location), choose a folder from the Location pop-up menu.

To pick a folder other than those listed in the Location menu, choose Choose a Folder and then click the Choose button.

6 Click Create. The collage is created and stored in the specified location on disk.

extra bits

save image as Desktop p. 108

- After creating a Picasabackground file, you can change the way it's displayed by choosing a different Position option (such as Stretch or Center) in the Display Properties dialog box.

create a screen saver p. 109

- When selecting images for a screen saver, you'll probably prefer to use larger pictures that fill the screen. Smaller or cropped photos will be surrounded by black bands.

- To replace the Picasa screensaver with a new one, delete all images in the Screensaver folder and then perform the same steps using a new set of photos.

- If you later want to restore your previous screen saver or select a new one, open the Display control panel, click the Screen Saver tab, select a screen saver, click Apply, and then click OK.

make a movie p. 110

- Unless a movie will contain many pictures, set the Delay between pictures to a high number, such as 4 or 5 seconds. Smaller numbers will cause the images to quickly disappear offscreen.

- Experiment with the listed codecs until you find one that gives you consistently good results; that is, a small movie (in KB) with clear images. Note, however, that the ability of others to view the movie depends on them having the same codec installed on their computer.

- There's no Picasa option to name a movie. To change a movie's name, right-click its Windows file icon, choose Rename, and edit the name. Click a blank area of the Desktop when finished.

create a poster p. 112

- Larger, high-resolution photos will result in better posters than smaller, low-resolution photos.

- The greater the enlargement percentage you choose, the more images/pages will result.

make a collage p. 113

- To create a new Desktop from a collage, choose Save as Desktop Picture from the Location pop-up menu and click Create. Click Yes in the Confirm dialog box that appears.

9. saving and backing up photos

If you modify an image in Picasa (changing the contrast, effects, and so on), your edits are only visible when the image is viewed in Picasa. The program never alters your original pictures; it merely makes note of the changes you've made. While this ensures that you don't inadvertently alter your original photos, it can make things difficult if you want to share the pictures with others (who may use a different program for editing and viewing images) or if you want to do additional editing in another program.

To simplify the process of sharing your pictures, opening them in other programs or on other platforms, and backing them up for safekeeping, Picasa provides four procedures. See the table below for a quick summary of the purposes and differences between them. We'll discuss each of these procedures in depth.

Procedure	Description
Save a Copy	Save a Picasa-edited image as a new file that can be viewed, edited, or printed with any program. All files (regardless of their original format) are saved as JPEGs.
Export Picture to Folder	Save any pictures (edited or not) to a folder as new JPEGs. You can optionally change the size and amount of compression.
Create a Gift CD	Copy selected folders to CD or DVD as JPEGs for display on another computer; can optionally include a copy of Picasa and a Windows program to display the images as a slideshow.
Backup Pictures	Back up photo folders to CD, DVD, or another hard disk. Images are backed up without modification, although Picasa edits are separately noted and retained.

save a copy

Edits made to photos using Picasa's tools are only visible within Picasa. The simplest way to create a copy of an edited image that can be viewed or printed with any program is to use the Save a Copy command.

1 Open the photo for editing or select its thumbnail in the Picture Library.

2 Choose File > Save a Copy ($\boxed{\text{Ctrl}}$ $\boxed{\text{S}}$).

What happens next depends on the file you selected for copying:

If the file has never been edited in Picasa, no copy is made.

If the file has been edited and is any file type other than a JPEG (.jpg), a copy of the file is saved in the same folder using the same name but with the type and extension .jpg. For example, Birds.tif would result in a Birds.jpg file.

If the file has been edited and is a JPEG (.jpg) file, a copy of the file is saved in the same folder with a sequential number added to the base filename. For example, Birds.jpg would result in a Birds1.jpg file.

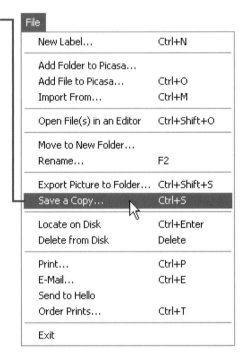

Whether the copy will instantly appear in the Picture Library depends on the Folder Manager setting for the destination folder. If the folder is set for Watch for Changes, copies will automatically appear. To make copies appear in a folder set for Scan Once, choose Folder > Refresh Thumbnails or choose this command from the folder's Actions button menu (found in the Picture Library to the right of the folder name).

export to folder

If you want control over the image quality, size, and destination folder of copies, use the Export Picture to Folder command rather than Save a Copy. Like Save a Copy, Export Picture to Folder automatically saves (and converts, if necessary) all images to JPEG (.jpg) format. However, Export Picture to Folder can create a copy of any picture—not just the ones you've edited with Picasa.

1 In the Picture Library, select the picture or pictures you want to export.

To select multiple pictures, you can Ctrl-click individual pictures, drag a selection rectangle around a contiguous group, Shift-click the first and last picture in a contiguous group, or choose Edit > Select All (Ctrl A). To include pictures from multiple folders, select pictures from the first folder, click the Hold button, select additional pictures from a different folder, and so on.

2 Choose File > Export Picture to Folder (Ctrl Shift S). The Export to Folder dialog box appears.

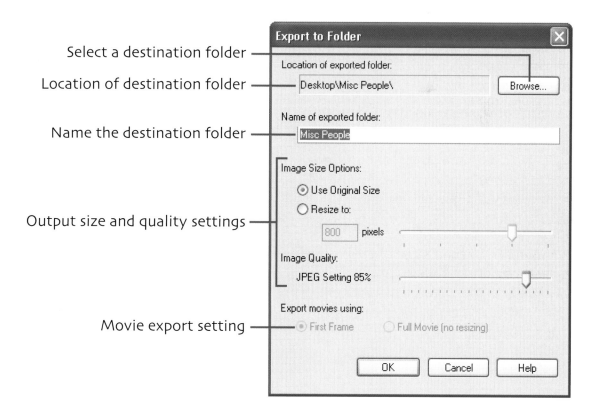

Select a destination folder

Location of destination folder

Name the destination folder

Output size and quality settings

Movie export setting

export to folder (cont.)

3 In the Export to Folder dialog box, specify the name and location of the export folder.

To set the name of the export folder, you can either accept the default name in the Name of exported folder box (the original folder's name) or change the name in the box to one of your choosing.

To set the location for the export folder, click Browse, select a folder in the Browse for Folder dialog box, and click OK. (The new folder will be created inside of the selected folder or location.)

4 Specify the desired maximum size of the exported images.

To export the images unaltered, click the Use Original Size radio button.

To make the exported pictures a specific size, click the Resize to radio button. Then enter a number in the text box (in pixels) or drag the slider to reflect the desired size. (Pictures smaller than the specified size will be exported unaltered—in their original size. Pictures that are larger than the specified size will be reduced so that their largest dimension matches the target size.)

5 Drag the Image Quality slider to set the amount of compression to be applied to the exported pictures. The lower the Image Quality setting, the greater the loss of data and clarity.

6 Click OK. The selected pictures are exported as new JPEG files, and then the destination folder is opened for you.

saving and backing up photos

create a gift CD

If you want to give copies of your favorite photos to a friend or relative (or simply transfer them to a different computer), you can use the Create a Gift CD command. A gift CD can contain any combination of folders and labels. The resulting normal JPEG files can be opened and viewed on almost any computer, such as other Windows, Mac, and Linux machines.

1 In the Picture Library, display one of the folders or labels that you want to include on the CD. Then click the Gift CD button at the top of the window or choose Folder > Create a Gift CD. The bottom section of the window changes to display CD-creation options.

CD options

create a gift CD (cont.)

2 To add other folders and labels to the CD or to remove the initial folder or label, click the Add More button in Section 1.

3 The Folders on Disk list appears (on the left side of the window). Add and remove check marks as necessary. Checked folders and labels will be copied to the CD.

4 Optional: To resize the pictures, choose a size (in pixels) from the Picture Size pop-up menu in Section 1. Images larger than the chosen size will be reduced to the new size.

5 Optional: If the CD will be opened on a PC, you can check the Include Slideshow check box in Section 1. Doing so will include software that will automatically display the CD's pictures as a slideshow whenever the disk is inserted. (If you're sending the disk to a Mac or Linux user, you can skip this option.)

6 Enter a name for the CD in the CD Name text box in Section 2. The name will appear in Windows Explorer/My Computer when viewed on a PC or on the desktop of a Mac.

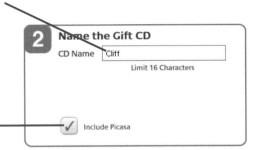

7 Optional: If the recipient is a PC user who you think would like a copy of the Picasa 2 software, check the Include Picasa check box in Section 2. (If you're sending the disk to a Mac or Linux user, you can skip this option.)

saving and backing up photos

8 Click the Burn Disc button (to the right of Section 2). When requested, insert a blank disc in your CD or DVD burner and close the drive door. Click the Write button to burn the CD or DVD.

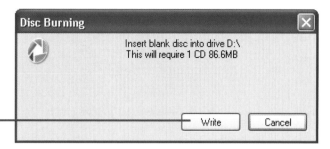

A pop-up box appears on the right side of the Picasa screen, showing the progress of the CD/DVD burning.

9 When your CD or DVD is ready, this dialog box appears. Click the Eject button to retrieve the finished disc.

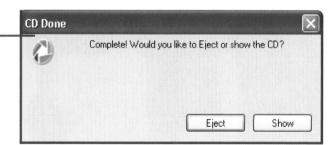

archive photos

To safeguard your photos from drive failure, fire, and other catastrophes, Picasa has a Backup Pictures routine that you can use to archive photos to CD, DVD, or another hard drive. Backup Pictures copies the original files, as well as noting any edits you've made in Picasa. Because Backup Pictures also places a restore program (PicasaRestore.exe) on the backup disc or drive, you can also use Backup Pictures to move copies of your files to another PC.

Backups are created as named sets. Each set keeps track of all files that have already been backed up, enabling you to perform incremental backups in which only new and changed files are recorded in subsequent backups.

1 Choose Tools > Backup Pictures or click the Backup button at the top of the window. The bottom section of the window presents backup options; the left side displays the Folders on Disk list.

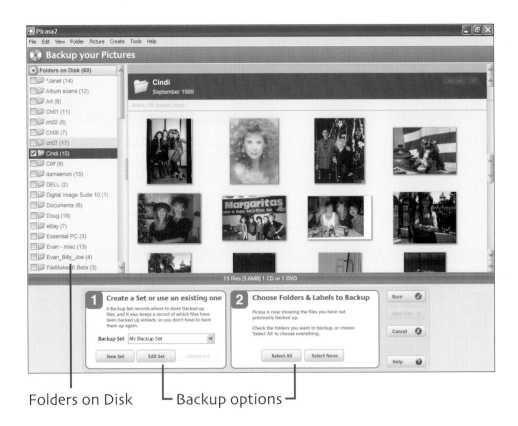

Folders on Disk   └ Backup options ┘

2 On your first backup of a particular set of folders, click the New Set button. The New Backup Set dialog box appears.

3 Enter a name for the backup set, indicate the backup type (to CD/DVD or to another drive), and specify the file types to back up. (If backing up to a hard disk, click Choose to select the drive.) Click Create to continue.

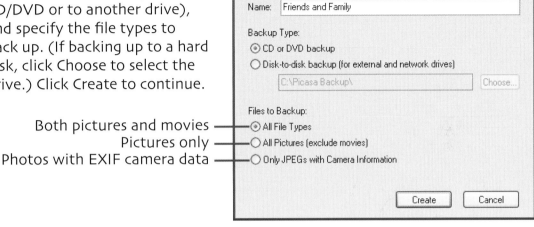

Both pictures and movies ——— All File Types
Pictures only ——— All Pictures (exclude movies)
Photos with EXIF camera data ——— Only JPEGs with Camera Information

4 In the Folders on Disk list (see previous page), click check boxes of all folders to be backed up.

To perform a complete backup, click the Select All button in Section 2. To start over (clearing the check boxes of all selected folders), click Select None.

5 To create the backup, click the Burn button (to the right of Section 2).

If backing up to a hard drive, the backup begins immediately. If backing up to CD or DVD, insert a blank CD or DVD when prompted and then click Write. (Note that you will be asked to insert a new blank CD or DVD for each backup; you cannot reuse your existing backup discs.)

6 CD/DVD backup only: When prompted, click the Eject button to complete the backup.

saving and backing up photos   **123**

extra bits

save a copy p. 116

- The Save a Copy command has no options. No dialog box appears when saving a copy of a file in this manner. You can't specify a filename or select a destination folder, for example.

- You can also use the Save a Copy command to simultaneously make copies of multiple pictures. Before issuing the command, (Ctrl)-click each picture that you want to copy. (When selecting pictures to copy, use Hold to add pictures from multiple folders.)

export to folder p. 117

- JPEG files use lossy compression. That is, the higher the compression you select, the more image quality you'll lose. (By comparison, compression algorithms for TIFF files are lossless. That is, no image quality is lost; the files are simply made smaller.) If you're exporting digital photos that will only be viewed onscreen, you can safely apply much higher compression before its effects are evident onscreen. However, if you intend to print the exported files or edit them in another program, you'll want to keep compression to a minimum—use a JPEG setting close to 100%.

- If you've previously exported images from the current folder, you can select the previous destination folder. Doing so prevents the creation of a new subfolder.

create a gift CD p. 119

- Gift CDs reflect edits you've made in Picasa. The resulting images can be viewed in any program— not just Picasa.

- When creating a Gift CD, Picasa tells you how much data will be written and the number of discs required. A blank CD holds approximately 650 MB. If you're over that amount, you can pick a smaller image size or reduce the number of images by selecting fewer folders.

archive photos p. 122

- The advantage of backing up to a hard disk is that it occurs immediately; no disc shuffling is required. The disadvantage is that if something happens to your computer—it's stolen or destroyed, for example—your backups will be lost, too.

saving and backing up photos

- To later add new and changed files to an existing backup set (performing an incremental backup), choose Tools > Backup Pictures or click the Backup button. Select the set name from the Backup Set drop-down menu, and click Burn.

- When performing subsequent backups to the same set, you can add more folders by clicking their check boxes.

- When you insert a CD or DVD backup into a PC, PicasaRestore automatically runs. You can restore the files to their original locations or to a new folder. To stop the restoration, click Cancel.

- To restore a backup made to a hard drive, open the backup folder on that drive and run the copy of PicasaRestore you find there.

- If you want to move Picasa-edited photos to a Mac or Linux system, use the Create a Gift CD procedure rather than Backup.

- To delete a backup set, issue the Backup Pictures command, select the set name from the Backup Set drop-down list, and click Delete Set. (Note that if you've been backing up to a hard drive, this does not delete the backup data, too. Quit Picasa and manually delete the files.)

10. sharing photos with Hello

Hello is a free one-on-one chat and picture-sharing application you can use in conjunction with Picasa. Unlike using email to send images to one another, Hello has no file-size limit. You can send full-size, high-resolution photos without worrying about anything other than the required transmission time. And if you have a broadband connection (a cable or DSL Internet account), even that isn't an issue. In this chapter, you'll learn the basics of using Hello as a Picasa adjunct.

start a Hello session

Because they're generally used together, you'll normally want to launch both Hello and Picasa at the start of each session. You can launch them individually or perform an action in one that causes the other to launch. For example, selecting files in Picasa and clicking the Hello button results in Hello launching.

1 Launch Picasa and Hello. Depending on the options selected when you installed Hello and settings you've chosen in its Options dialog box, you can launch Hello in the following ways:

- Choose Hello from the Start > Programs menu.
- If Hello is set to automatically run when Windows starts, right-click its System Tray icon and choose Show.
- If you installed a Desktop shortcut or a Quick Launch icon (found at the left end of the taskbar) for Hello, click the icon.
- From within Picasa, select one or more images you want to transmit, and then choose File > Send to Hello or click the Hello button.

2 If you've configured your account to automatically log in whenever you launch Hello, this login dialog box appears briefly and is replaced by the Hello window.

Otherwise, enter your Hello password (if it isn't already filled in) and click the Sign-In button. Hello's window appears (see page 127).

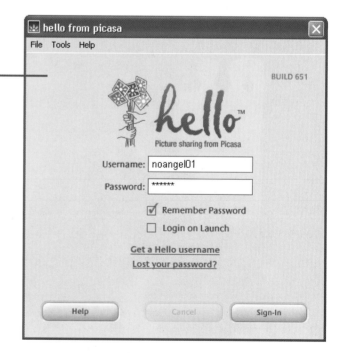

sharing photos with Hello

prepare for chat

Before you start your first Hello session, you may want to set preferences in the Options dialog box. The most important settings are explained below.

Logging in. To automate the Hello login process, check the options to Remember my password and Automatically log in. If you use Hello constantly, you may want to check Launch Hello when Windows starts. Otherwise, leave it unchecked.

Picture Sizes and Bandwidth. If you have dial-up Internet (rather than cable or DSL), you may want to enable and enter a number for the Maximum width/height of sent pictures. Start with 800 or smaller and adjust the setting after sending a few large test images.

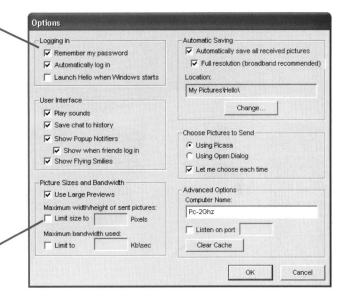

Options dialog box

Automatic Saving. Depending on the number of megapixels your friends' cameras have and whether their images are raw, compressed, or resized, digital photos can sometimes be immense. If you have a dial-up connection, you may want to remove the check mark from Full resolution (broadband recommended). Doing so causes all pictures to be sent to you in a reduced size, suite mainly for onscreen viewing. If you receive photos you want to print, you can request that full-resolution versions of them by sent to you by following the instructions on page 133.

Location. To specify a different folder in which to save incoming photos, click the Change button.

Choose Pictures to Send. You can select pictures to send in Picasa, Windows (Use Open Dialog), or both. Set the preferred method of selecting a picture source. If you click Let me choose each time, a dialog box will appear each time you initiate a send.

start a session

After launching Hello, you can start a session with a friend by double-clicking her or his name in the Online list on Hello's opening screen. A new tab appears for your friend at the top of the window. You can now chat and exchange photos.

Current chat friend's tab   Image friend is viewing   Chat window

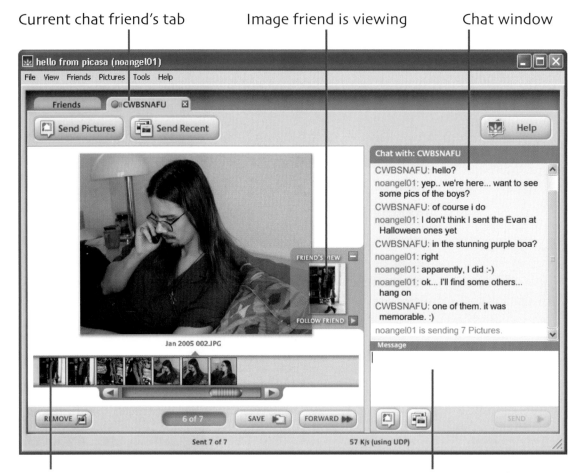

Filmstrip of images sent and received in the current session

Type new chat text here and click Send.

sharing photos with Hello

send pictures

You can send pictures from within Picasa, from Hello, or from Windows by performing the steps on this and the following pages.

Send pictures from Picasa

1 In Picasa, select the images you want to send (see Chapter 3). The selected images will appear in Picasa's Picture Tray.

2 Choose File > Send to Hello or click the Hello button.

3 The Select the friends to send pictures to dialog box appears. Click the name of the friend who will receive the pictures. (To select more than one person, Ctrl-click their names). Click the Send button.

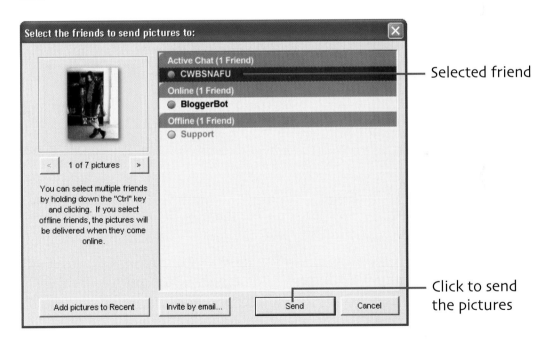

Selected friend

Click to send the pictures

The pictures are added to the filmstrip area of the Hello window (see page 130). Transmission begins immediately for online friends. If any of the selected people are offline, the pictures will be sent to them the next time they run Hello.

send pictures (cont.)

Send pictures from Hello

1 In Hello, click the Send Pictures button. Depending on your settings for the Choose Pictures to Send options (see page 129), Picasa will appear, a Send Picture dialog box will open, or a Locate Pictures using dialog box will appear.

2 If Use Picasa is clicked or is the default setting, Picasa appears. Select pictures and then click the Hello button.

If Use Explorer is clicked or Use Open Dialog is the default setting, select image files in the Send Picture dialog box and then click Open. (To select multiple files, [Ctrl]-click each filename before clicking the Open button.)

3 Pick recipients in the Select the friends to send pictures to dialog box (see page 131) and click Send. The selected images are immediately transmitted to all online recipients and held for offline recipients.

If you enabled the Let me choose each time option, this dialog box appears. Click a button.

Send Picture dialog box

Drag-and-drop files from Windows

When you send pictures using any of the previously described procedures, non-JPEG files are automatically changed to JPEGs before transmission.

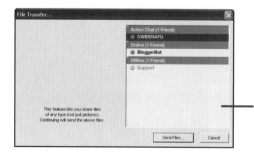

To send images in other formats (TIFF, for example) or to send non-image files (such as word processing or worksheet documents), drag their file icons onto the Hello window. When you release the mouse button, a File Transfer dialog box appears. To send the file(s), select recipients and click the Send Files button.

sharing photos with Hello

receive pictures

Receiving files in Hello couldn't be easier. In fact, it requires no action at all on the recipient's part; the files just arrive. And as long as Automatically save all received pictures is checked in the Options dialog box, incoming picture files are automatically saved in the folder specified in the same dialog box.

If you're a Picasa user, images received in Hello are stored in Picasa's From Hello collection. A subcollection and folders for each friend are created within the collection.

If necessary, you can manually save the current picture. Click the Save button at the bottom of the screen. In the dialog box that appears, select a destination folder for the picture, change its filename (if you wish), and click Save.

Save selected image

If Full resolution (broadband recommended) is not enabled in Hello's Options dialog box (see page 129), all received images will be low-resolution. While suitable for viewing onscreen, such pictures may print poorly. To request an original, full-resolution copy of a received image, follow these steps:

1 In Picasa, open the received image in Edit View.

2 To request the transmission of the original, full-resolution picture, click the Get Highres button above the image. The original image is transmitted to you.

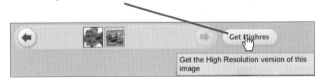

extra bits

start a session p. 130

- To chat and swap photos with friends, they must be Hello users. You can encourage them to get Hello by clicking the Invite button. Enter their email addresses in the Invite Friends dialog box. Hello will either tell you they're currently registered or offer to send them an invitation by email.

- To add a current Hello user to your Friends list, click the Add Friend button and then enter his or her user name.

- To remove the tab of a person with whom you've finished chatting, make the tab active and then click the tiny x.

- Hello saves a history of your chat sessions. To review a session, select the user's name in the left side of the Hello window. Then double-click the session entry in the Shared History list.

send pictures p. 131

- After sending pictures to one person, you may decide to share them with another online friend. Click the Send Recent button. Thumbnails of all recently sent images are shown. Select the ones you want to send to your current chat friend and click the Send to Friend button.

- You can share received pictures with other friends. Select a picture, click the Forward button, select recipients, and click Send.

- If you have a Blogger blog (Web log), you can use Hello to upload pictures from Picasa to the blog. For instructions, choose Help > Hello Online Help. Click the link labeled "Post a Picture to a Blog."

- If you have a webcam, you can snap a picture of yourself and send it through Hello by choosing Tools > Webcam/DV Capture.

- You can also send a picture of the active window or your screen. Right-click the Hello icon in the System Tray and choose Send Picture of Window or Send Picture of Screen.

receive pictures p. 133

- After receiving some photos, you can quickly find them on disk or in Picasa. Right-click the active image in Hello, and then choose Locate Picture on Disk or Locate Picture in Picasa from the pop-up menu (see page 127).

- During a chat session, you can eliminate some of the clutter in the filmstrip area by choosing a Pictures > Remove command.

sharing photos with Hello

index

index

index

index

index

V

Video Compression dialog box, 110
Visual QuickProject Guides, ix

W

Wal-Mart Digital Photo Center, 102
wallpaper, 108
Warmify effect, 83
Watch for Changes option, Folder Manager, 55, 61, 66, 116
watched folders, 61
Web graphics, 25
Web logs, 1. See also blogs
Web page, displaying photos on, xii, 111
webcams, 63–64, 134
Windows Explorer, 66, 120
Windows Media Player, 110
Windows systems
    and automatic media detection, 21, 63
    and gift CDs, 119
    and Initial Picture Scan option, 29
    installing Picasa on, 4
    sending images from, 131, 132
Wolf Camera, 102

Z

Zoom icons, 19
zoom slider, 17, 19

Ready to Learn More?

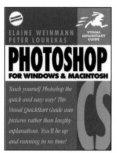